MW01226785

We Shall Be Like Him

We Shall Be Like Him

Bonnie B. Robinson

Bonfire Press, LC
Salt Lake City, UT

Bonfire Press, LC
171 East Third Avenue, #708
Salt Lake City, UT 84103
www.bonfirepress.com

Copyright © 2007 Bonnie B. Robinson
First printing, June 2007
Printed in the United States of America

Cover art: "Mary and the Resurrected Lord" by Harry Anderson
© by Intellectual Reserve, Inc.
Used by permission

Cover design: © 2007 Bonfire Press, LC
Photograph of the author is courtesy of Eric Bjorklund, Acclaim Photography

All rights reserved.
No part of this book may be used or reproduced in any manner whatsoever, including but not limited to reproduction by electronic means, photocopying or other imaging devices, or by any information storage or retrieval system, without the prior written permission of Bonfire Press, LC. The only exception is that brief quotes may be included in a book review or a personal journal, if they are framed in quotation marks and include the full title of the book, *We Shall Be Like Him*.
The thoughts expressed herein are the author's views and do not necessarily represent the position of The Church of Jesus Christ of Latter-day Saints, nor any other institution or organization.

ISBN–13: 978-1-931858-12-0

To my parents,
Mark J. and Elma S. Bradshaw.

Wherefore,... pray unto the Father
with all the energy of heart,
that ye may be filled with this love,...
that when he shall appear
we shall be like him.
Moroni 7:48

Acknowledgements

A huge *thank you* goes to those who pre-read this manuscript and freely offered me support and encouragement: my husband, Glenn Robinson, my friends Barbara Smith and Kathleen Anderson, and especially Karlene Browning for her skilled editing.

I love and appreciate my four children, their spouses, and my grandchildren, who put up with my fanatacism in finishing this laborious, yet joyful, project.

I'm grateful for prophets and apostles—ancient and modern—who reveal the word of God to the inhabitants of earth. Also, I'm thankful for access to the inspired writings, speeches, and examples of many other influencial individuals too numerous to name. I feel blessed beyond measure to be a member of The Church of Jesus Christ of Latter-day Saints.

Foremost, I express my gratitude to God the Eternal Father, who gave my spirit life, and to my Savior Jesus Christ, whose infinite atonement offers salvation and spiritual rebirth, and to the Holy Ghost, whose witness of truth has rendered an indelible testimony in my soul.

Contents

Prologue   ix

1 That They All May Be One   1

2 Fullness   17

3 Grace for Grace   31

4 About My Father's Business   47

5 Increase Our Faith   61

6 The Truth Shall Make You Free   77

7 The Resurrection and the Life   93

8 Inherit the Kingdom of God   105

9 More, Savior, Like Thee   125

10 We Shall Be Like Him   139

   Bibliography   155

   Index   157

chapters

Prologue

At first it seemed surreal, as if this were a three-dimensional movie. Right before my eyes stood the sign for the Garden Tomb, outside the walled city of Jerusalem. With a BYU tour to the Holy Land, I had been appointed as "tribe scribe" to chronicle our two-week trip and distribute the record to our group. While scribbling sentences in my notebook, I followed our guide toward a bench-lined gazebo, where lavender bougainvilleas draped the roof. Until then, bougainvilleas weren't part of my vocabulary, and even now my computer spell checker is in shock with such a dramatic word. The mellow aroma of the blossoms mingled with other sweet scents in the spring-green garden.

Within the gazebo, I settled onto a wooden bench amid our tour group. My heart hiccupped when I saw the nearby hill called Calvary. *Incredible!* I thought. *I'm actually here where Jesus died. This is real—not a TV documentary—but an authentic live broadcast from my senses to my soul. Time for a spirituality upgrade. Forget about world peace. Just aim for peace in your own heart.*

Though a pang of sorrow creased my soul, I continued to stare at the oft-photographed outcropping of rocks that resembled a skull. Calgary. Golgotha. Much more than mere names. This was the hallowed, yet fearful, place where soldiers nailed Jesus to a cross of wood—the very spot where eternal life and salvation hung in the balance. *Time to surrender,* I decided. *Put up the white flag. Jesus has forever won my soul. He is always victorious. Truly, He has overcome all things, including my stubborn human nature.*

Atop the hill stood telephone poles, like symbolic crosses on which our Savior and two thieves were crucified. A sacred site. A holy hill in the Holy Land. After touring Israel for six days, I felt anchored with a tangible grasp of Jesus' life on earth. But now the impact of His death scalded my mind—His anguish, sacrifice, suffering—His priceless and infinite atonement. A lump of sorrow choked my throat.

Our guide began to relate the account of Christ's final hours on earth. Beneath the ebb and flow of his words, my self-examination mushroomed. *Why had I sat down? I should be on my feet pacing. Or better yet, on my knees repenting.* I stood up, offered my seat to someone else, then leaned against a pillar on a shadowed edge of the gazebo, where I could conceal my weeping.

Behind me drifted a soft hymn, sung by another group in the garden. I didn't understand their foreign words, yet their music reverenced this hallowed place.

Though I could no longer see Calvary, my tour group still gazed upon the fateful hillside. Despite the suffusive tranquility of the garden and the soft-spoken words of our guide, no one dozed off, as had occurred earlier in the week due to our jet lag. Today's red-rimmed eyes were not from fatigue, but from humble tears of gratitude.

The guide gestured to the far corner of the garden where we would soon view the treasured tomb. *So close! Why am I just standing here? My feet aren't super-glued to the stone pavement.* An unseen force began to tug on me. Still endeavoring to jot down the words of our guide, I edged away from the gazebo. Then I tiptoed past the singing foreigners, whose hymn faded with a series of "amens." Enveloped in the garden's peace, I felt cocooned in comfort as

I followed the short path toward the sacred sepulcher. Rustling leaves overhead whispered that I was getting close.

My footsteps halted on a tree-shadowed overlook, where I glanced down at the stone-carved sepulcher. My breathing ceased. I could no longer take notes. I dared not move nor do anything to disturb the profound moment.

A surge of spiritual power thrust through my heart and made it pound like a tom-tom. I folded my hands and pressed my notebook against my chest to contain the throbbing. The Spirit warmed me with a vivid witness: *Jesus was carried here after His death on the cross. He was laid in this tomb, then arose on the third day.*

With one quivering hand, I covered my mouth that wanted to shout "Hallelujah!" My eyes could not unfasten their gaze on the rectangular hole, once covered by a rolling stone. *Though this tomb now stood empty, it was not without life. Bursting forth in glorious resurrection, Jesus Christ became the source of eternal life. Then He showed us the pathway home to our Father.*

I could barely keep my knees from buckling—not only from their quaking, but also because I sensed the need to pray—worshiping in gratitude for the miracle of divine rebirth. My thumping heart increased its speed. Unbelievable thoughts jammed in my mind. *Jesus has been in this garden! He actually stood here long ago. And He is here again! Right now! Right behind you! Just turn around!*

I took in a trembling breath. *Did I dare look? Had I prepared myself to be in Christ's presence? Was there a dress code? A behavior code? Should I smile and look into His face, or fall humbly at His feet?* With both anxiety and reverence, I slowly rotated my head to glance over my shoulder. Certain He was close, I blinked several times in an effort to see Him. But no one was there. Only trees and flowers and stones amid the garden.

Although I did not view Him in person, I felt drenched in His merciful love. And then, as faint as a snowflake striking a windowpane, I heard a sound. *Was it my name? Did a hushed voice speak my name, just as Mary Magdalene had heard her name near this Garden Tomb?* I wasn't certain. Yet how I wished it were true! Even as I write this, I still yearn for the day when Jesus calls my name and beckons me to come near.

I didn't want that moment of pure love to end! But alas, the Garden Tomb was a public place, and within a few minutes I found myself swept back into the midst of our tour group. I followed them down a set of stairs to get a closer look at the tomb. While awaiting my turn to enter, I pondered the story of when "[Mary] saw Jesus standing and knew not that it was Jesus" (John 20:14). Then I wondered, will I know Jesus well enough to recognize Him when I see Him?

Might He ask me, as He did Mary, "Woman, why weepest thou? whom seekest thou?" (v. 15). Could I honestly reply that I'm seeking Jesus every day of my life? Is He the focus of all my words and acts? Do I yearn to learn more and more about Him? How can I qualify to stand in His presence? Do I feel an eagerness to become like Him?

> "If you really want to *be* like the Lord—more than any *thing* or *anyone* else—you must remember that your adoration of Jesus is best shown by your emulation of Him." [Russell M. Nelson, "Endure and Be Lifted Up," *Ensign*, May 1997, 72, italics in the original.]

Never before, and never after that soul-filling day at the Garden Tomb, have I experienced such a profound encounter with the Divine. Now I long to recapture that indescribable sense of joy, peace, and the pure love of Christ. How I yearn to offer those heaven-sent emotions with others. That's the message of this book: to feel and share the pure love of Christ as we journey on a heart-energizing quest to become like Him.

> Wherefore,... pray unto the Father with all the energy of heart, that ye may be filled with this love,... that when he shall appear *we shall be like him*" (Moroni 7:48, emphasis added).

That they all may be one;
as thou, Father, art in me, and I in thee,
that they also may be one in us.
John 17:21

That They All May Be One

First a disclaimer: Reading this chapter will not instantly make you one with God. Nor will reading this entire book. Extraordinary spirituality doesn't evolve in the blink of an eye. Don't worry if you start to read this book and never finish. No one will give you electric shock therapy. Furthermore, if you do read it but don't feel edified, that's my fault as an author, so no one will perform a lobotomy on your brain. However, remember that as the reader, you can enhance your personal enlightenment through pondering and prayer. With those pronouncements in place, we may begin.

How marvelous is the oneness of God the Father and Jesus Christ, who said, "I and my Father are one" (John 10:30). "I am in the Father, and the Father in me, and the Father and I are one" (D&C 93:3). Latter-day revelation has clarified these verses:

> I do not apprehend that any intelligent person will construe these words to mean that Jesus and his Father are one person, but merely that they are one in knowledge, in truth, in wisdom, in understanding, and in purpose; just as the Lord Jesus himself admonished his disciples to be one with him, and to be in him,

that he might be in them.... I declare to you that they are not one person, but that they are two persons, two bodies, separate and apart, and as distinct as are any father and son within the sound of my voice. [Joseph F. Smith *Gospel Doctrine,* 68]

As our spiritual brother, Jesus has asked our Father that "even as many as will believe on my name, that they may become the sons [and daughters] of God, even one in me as I am one in the Father, as the Father is one in me, that we may be one" (D&C 35:2).

> That they all may be one; as thou, Father, art in me, and I in thee, that they also may be one in us:...
> And the glory which thou gavest me I have given them; that they may be one, even as we are one:
> I in them, and thou in me, that they may be made perfect in one (John 17:11,20–23).

Perfect in one with the Father and Son! How humbling to think such Hallowed Beings desire for us to become one with Them! For me that seems like quite a stretch. I may need something akin to a torture rack from the Middle Ages to extend me toward godliness. I might also need cardiovascular surgery to achieve the required mighty change of heart (see Mosiah 5:2).

What Oneness Is

During our oldest son's two-year mission, he not only developed spiritual prowess, but he also physically matured to reach his father's stature. One Sunday as he walked beside his dad after sacrament meeting, a man they followed turned around to see them. As he studied the likeness of this father and son, one word fell from the man's lips, "Clones!"

In the science arena, a clone becomes an exact replica of the same animal. In the case of my son, he had developed into a replica of his father, but only through genetics and not scientific experimentation. Adding to their likeness of appearance, my husband claims that our son thinks in the same manner as he does, and therefore they share a unique unity in our family. This is similar to Christ's precise likeness to God the Father. Their oneness of thought, resemblance in appearance, and similarity of attributes make the Father and Son fully united in power and purpose.

> They are one—in attributes. They are one in love, one in knowledge, one in mercy, one in power, one in all things that make them united and powerful, glorious and great, because in them is perfected all truth, all virtue and all righteousness. [Joseph F. Smith, *Collected Discourses Delivered by President Wilford Woodruff, His Two Counselors, the Twelve Apostles, and Others, 5 Volumes,* 4:66.]

Believe it or not, the inhabitants of earth can become one with God the Father and Jesus Christ. But only if we acquire the divine attributes that unite us in celestial glory with Them.

Perfection Is Possible

During the Sermon on the Mount, Jesus admonished, "Be ye therefore perfect, even as your Father which is in heaven is perfect" (Matthew 5:48). The footnote translates "perfect" into the Greek, meaning "complete, finished, fully developed." I personally prefer the idea of being finished and complete to the laborious task of perfection.

I also like the adage, "The task ahead of us is never as great as the Power behind us." Of course, sublime power emanates from the throne of God. We make jokes about needing to be struck by lightning before we'll repent and improve; however, godly characteristics are not learned in a flash.

That reminds me of a story told by a recently returned missionary. On his first day in the Philippines, he and his companion were caught in a deluge of rain. The companion quickly ushered him under an awning to escape getting wet. Unfortunately, the awning was metal, and this missionary was tall enough that his head made contact with it. Then, zing! A flash of lightning struck the awning! The brand new missionary got knocked out cold.

Gratefully, he was not burned or hurt, as might have been the case. But he did comment that his initial experience as a missionary was much more poignant than his initiation into a college fraternity. In order to avoid any future lightning bolts, he became a dedicated and serious servant of God.

Is our emergence toward godliness an emergency? Perhaps it is. As I see it, the more I evolve into a Christlike being while on earth, the less time I'll have to spend in detox and rehabilitation in the spirit world.

Wholeness and holiness are meant for everyone. "And ye shall be holy unto me: for I the Lord am holy" (Leviticus 20:26). This, of course, rarely occurs within the span of mortal life, except in rare individuals like Elijah, who was translated into glory. To achieve oneness with the Father and Son means keeping an eternal perspective, as Joseph Smith taught, "When [God's] commandments teach us, it is in view of eternity; for we are looked upon by God as though we were in eternity; God dwells in eternity, and does not view things as we do." [*History of the Church*, Deseret Book Co., Salt Lake City, Utah, 1978, 6:313.]

Okay. That means *eternity is now*—not some distant goal. Each moment is part of the everlasting span of the Father's plan for His children. Thus, we short-change ourselves to think were are merely human beings. Rather, we are spiritual entities temporarily separated from our heavenly home. Though Satan goads us with discouragement and reminds us of our flaws, God encourages us to keep driving along the road to perfection. His way is the Highway. It's best to regard our mortal lives through the clear windshield of eternity.

An Eternal Perspective

Stranded alone on a cliff one day, I learned a stunning lesson about God's eternal perspective. What was I doing, you might ask, dangling on the edge of a cliff with my hands clutching a bristlecone pine tree? Wasn't my life enough of a challenge with four teenagers to raise? My hands began to slip. I wedged one knee into the jagged shale wall. A chunk of rock broke loose and tumbled end over end toward a cluster of fir trees 600 feet below me. I would have given anything to be back down there on safe ground!

This is not what I had anticipated during this September day in the Wasatch Mountains. Though I'd scheduled to hike with a friend, she cancelled because of illness. Being a risk-taker, I decided to make the trek alone. The autumn morning felt brisk as I climbed from the car, driven by my husband. He cautioned me to be careful in my solo hike, then he left to go to his job in Salt Lake. The trail head began in Big Cottonwood Canyon, then I would hike over the high mountain ridge and down to my car, parked in Little Cottonwood Canyon.

In the early-morning shadows, I saw owls swooping overhead in search of food. From tall evergreens, squirrels chattered and dropped pinecones to the ground. I picked up a tiny pine nut and crushed it between my teeth. Bad decision! The bitter taste of pine sap remained embedded in my tongue as I followed yesterday's footprints up the pathway.

After three and a half miles, I reached a broad field, forming a bowl at the base of a lofty mountain ridge. There the trail thinned amid the grass and wild flowers, then it faded to nothingness. Lest I be like the Israelites and wander forty years in the wilderness, I took a hiking book from my backpack and read, "A faint foot track marks the best route up the ridge." While studying the mountain cirque around the meadow, I spied a faint path, angling upward. Above the thin trail, vertical cliffs sprouted, making jagged stripes down the mountainside. Though the cliffs might put my life in jeopardy, I thought I could loop below their lower edges, then hike beyond them to reach a less-steep, grassy hillside. From there I could easily reach the mountaintop.

While struggling up the first half of the tilted path, I realized this trail was meant for deer or other four-footed animals, which I was not. As the angle sharpened, I had to lean into the slope and grab clumps of grass and weeds to keep from falling. Thistle thorns pricked my palms, so I bravely donned a pair of cotton gloves. At the same time, I wished for anti-gravity boots to stave off the downhill tug toward trouble if I slipped in the slightest.

When finally I neared the first ragged cliff, I easily looped around its lower edge, just as I'd planned. No problem, or so I thought, feeling my ego swell. Perhaps I should have remembered that "Pride goeth before destruction, and an haughty spirit before a fall" (Proverbs 16:18).

What I saw next made my knees clack together in dismay. Between me and the adjacent cliff was a threatening devil's slide twelve feet across. The precipitous gully was strewn with loose gravel and shattered stones—a death path, skidding all the way to the base of the ridge. Why had I not foreseen this distressing sight from the meadow below? A shudder of fear fanned across my back and shoulders. My nervous system blipped into override. My knees tried to buckle. I caught hold of a clump of grass with my gloved hands. I strained to steady my footing, while exhaustion unsteadied the rest of my frame. How I longed to shut my eyes, in hopes of reopening them to discover this was merely a bad dream!

"Think! Think" I told my brain. "What should I do? No way can I risk crossing the devil's slide! Nor do I dare retrace my steps down the sheer trail."

I'd been a hiker from the days of my early childhood—since I first toddled behind my parents and older sister on trails leading from picnic spots in the mountains. As three younger brothers joined the family, I hiked with them, then with the Girl Scouts, Young Women, friends, dates, and later my husband and our four children. Though I've occasionally been lost for brief moments on previous excursions, never had I confronted a situation like this!

I was experienced enough to know it's easier to strive upward on a steep incline rather than risk a tricky descent. So I examined the pair of cliffs above me and the devil's slide between them. Though still a hazard of unstable debris, the uphill chute was crisscrossed by thin tree roots poking from the base of the cliffs. I considered using the roots as a ladder with which I could pull myself upward. Just thirty feet above me I saw a spot that appeared more safe. There, the dangerous gully of gravel narrowed where the parallel cliffs jutted toward each other. I would need to wedge myself through the foot-wide gap to prevent my tumbling down the treacherous slope.

Tentatively, I stepped into the bedeviled slide and grasped the first dangling tree root. One hiking boot found a secure hold against a ragged rock. Then my second hand shot upward to snatch the next root on my makeshift ladder. I scraped my ankle while moving my second foot into an awkward sideways stance. Now there was no choice but to slowly go hand over hand and foot above foot to climb toward the refuge where the cliffs protruded.

Reaching the top of my ladder, I extended one gloved hand toward the cliff wall. If I could just get a firm grip on both sides, I could then tug myself up into the protected area. My right hand, still sheathed in the cotton glove, clutched the craggy rock and pulled. Chunks of shale crushed in my fingers and crashed at my feet. I tried once more to grab hold, and again the rocky layers crumbled and fell away. The texture reminded me of sandbox mud pies dried in the sunshine. An attempt with my left hand on the opposite craggy wall yielded similar results. Again and again I tried, first with my right hand, then the left. Again and again my hands broke off chunks of shale.

My hopes began to disintegrate, just like the rocks. My heart jackhammered in my chest as it pumped adrenalin to my toiling lungs and limbs. Five trembling minutes passed. Each attempt to grasp hold caused more shattering of shale. Dust flew in my face and I coughed repeatedly. My eyes watered and stung, but I refused to actually cry, because that would weaken my body and my resolve all the more.

This was worse than any nightmare I could imagine. It seemed I had the lead role in a cheap horror movie. Yet there were no handsome heros to rescue me.

With my feet still anchored on rungs of my tree root ladder, I leaned my torso flat against the steep slope and let my weary arms drop to my sides. One cheek pressed against the gravel while I tried to breathe deeply and rest. Yet the air was too grimy to be refreshing. Momentarily I closed my eyes. For some odd reason I remembered that I hadn't wiped up the milk one son spilled at breakfast. Why should that matter to me now? Because I wasn't going to make it home again? Would I be remembered as a poor housekeeper at my memorial services?

That thought somehow made me smile. Just because I was stuck on a devil's slide didn't mean the devil could force me to give up this battle. I had faith. I had courage. I'd overcome other tribulations during life and motherhood. Hadn't I helped four lively kids through dirty diapers (before disposables were popular), potty training, skinned knees, knocked out teeth, wounds that required stitches, and, even more recently, I'd survived three of them getting drivers' licenses in less than four years, with one son still to go. What were a few cliffs against all those threats to my sanity and well-being? I would persist and conquer this adversity! After all, one of my ancestors was William the Conqueror. I had conquering genes, didn't I?

Feeling calmer and braver, I opened my eyes, then lifted my head and inhaled. The dust had settled, and the gulp of fresh air invigorated me. I quickly took off my gloves in hopes that my bare hands could better grip the shattering shale. After a few fumbling attempts, one hand finally found a secure hold. Anchoring my second hand near the first, I got a firm enough grasp to pull myself upward. With my feet scrambling and treading gravel, I managed to ease my body through the foot-wide slot between the jutting walls. Air heaved in and out of my lungs as I leaned to rest against the inner edge of my newly-found sanctum. My legs quaked like spindly trees in the wind. Most of my fingernails were painfully broken to the quick. But for a moment I could truly relax—no longer in danger of the perilous devil's slide.

I found myself in a steeply-slanted, rock-hewn cubical about five feet square. The stone wall at my left, which I'd planned to go up and over to reach the grassy hillside, stood at least ten feet high with no ledges or footholds to use in my ascent. Warding off discouragement, I looked upward to my right. That wall of rock appeared to be eight feet high, but with more of a sloped angle that might be climbable. Yet one visible problem remained: the cliff was composed of the same unstable shale that had repeatedly shattered in my hands.

Then a glimmer of hope. Slightly above my head, a bristlecone pine tree grew from the side of the cliff. Though not more than three feet tall, the tree seemed to dare me to reach upward to it. First I braced both my feet, then I strained and stretched my right arm as high overhead as possible. Yes! I snatched one narrow branch. The thin needles crushed against my palm as I gave a hardy tug to test if the limb would hold my weight. I could almost hear the tree moan in protest. But with its roots fastened securely in the ledge, the tree appeared to withstand the strain. With eager arms, I pulled my body upward while my feet scrambled for secure spots on the shifty shelf of shale. Each attempted step loosened more rocks, which clattered down the mountainside.

With no sure footholds to keep me from slipping backwards, I thrust one hand up to clutch a second bristlecone pine trunk. As I pulled myself slightly higher on the cliff, I had no choice but to step on the first tree and smash it as I climbed. Thankfully, the trees didn't crumble beneath me like the rocks. Again I clawed my way upward, inching toward a third evergreen on the brink of the cliff. From there it was a sheer drop off in three directions. I carefully sat down, wrapped my shaky arms and legs around the skinny pine tree, and hung on.

Below me, I viewed the entire cirque of the mountain meadow, including the spot where I had safely stood an hour ago to scan this cliff. Why had I not discerned the immense danger awaiting me? Now I was stuck on a precipitous cliff and clinging to life by hugging a little pine tree! Pretty stupid. This elevation's thin atmosphere must have addled my brain.

Inhaling a surge of pine-scented air, my mind cleared and I began to see my environment with a new perspective. From this high pinnacle, I could better understand the Lord's view of our lives on earth. He perceives everything from a sublime vista. I should have prayed for God's guidance *before* venturing on this hike. I should have acknowledged His omniscience *in all things* before getting stranded on this cliff.

No longer would I try to go it alone. With my awkward grasp on the small tree, I couldn't kneel, but I could close my eyes, bow my head, and ask for divine sustenance to endure this self-imposed travail. After my prayer, I glanced around for angels to bear me up. No such luck. No instantaneous miracle. It was all up to me. Or was it?

One glance over my shoulder made me catch my breath. Along the spiny cliff grew a series of evergreens—white pines and bristlecones. Had God placed them there to be my lifeline? From where I sat, I could see only five or six trees in a row. I'd have to muster mighty faith to climb higher and hope the trees continued endlessly up the craggy cliff.

Clumsily, I got to my feet by wedging my boots against the base of the tree I'd been clinging to. Then I extended one hand toward a thick bough on the next evergreen. This pine tree was much hardier than the first three. That gave me confidence as I inched toward it. Then I had no choice but to brace myself in the middle of the scratchy limbs with the trunk at my back. From there I saw above me that tree after tree stood awaiting my grasp. Onward and upward I went, clutching needled limbs, tugging, toiling, towing my body upward. I trusted my life to these trees with their roots anchored in stone and their trunks growing straight toward heaven. Mostly I trusted their Creator. My Creator.

With the loose shale, my footings remained unsteady, and chunks of rock often skittered down the precipice. Sadly, I had to smash branches and break limbs as I steadied my hiking boots against the trees on my terrifying trek. It took a solid hour to ascend a mere 200 feet. Then the cliff melded into a grassy tundra.

With wobbly legs, I hiked the ridge to the final peak. My aching arms were scratched and bleeding from the endless poking twigs. My palms and fingers had blistered from grasping needled boughs. But I had made it to the top! I was alive!

Now I could kneel in prayer—this time in gratitude to God for the blessings and the lessons of the day. Never again will I venture through unfamiliar territory without first consulting Him. Each moment in time is precious, despite treacherous devil's slides and precipitous cliffs. Most of us can't discern what perils lie ahead on the pathways of life. Yet those who prayerfully tap into the Lord's eternal perspective can receive divine guidance to walk with Him.

As ye have therefore received Christ Jesus the Lord, so walk ye in him.

Rooted and built up in him, and stablished in the faith, as ye have been taught, abounding therein with thanksgiving (Colossians 2:6–7).

Rooted in Christ

The phrase "rooted in Christ" is not meant to imply cheering for Christ, although it seems we should root-a-toot-toot in joy over all He has done for us. Actually, being rooted in Christ is similar to how pine trees anchor their roots in the cliff's bedrock. Our spiritual roots must be firmly implanted in the "rock of our Redeemer, who is Christ, the Son of God" (Helaman 5:12). Only then can we stand tall and point ourselves straight toward heaven. And, like my lifeline of evergreen trees, we can then position ourselves to help others climb toward eternal life and exaltation.

During the early 1990's, colleagues at the University of Colorado theorized that the largest living organism in the world was a clump of aspen trees. [See Michael C. Grant, "The Trembling Giant," *Discover Magazine*, October 1993.] Though some people may conjecture that the largest living organism is a whale or a giant sequoia tree, scientific evidence shows that an aspen sends out horizontal shoots which take root and become new connected plants. The largest group is thought to be "A grove of aspen trees that fills 106 acres near Salt Lake City. All 47,000 stems sprout from the root of one tree. The grove, if hoisted, would weigh 13.2 million pounds." ["Loss of aspens worth quaking over," *Deseret Morning News*, August 6, 2006, G1.]

This interlinked series of trees is labeled as "one" plant. Though each tree has separate trunks, limbs, and leaves—each stands as an individual—their roots remain intertwined, making these aspens one enormous living organism. In a similar manner, humans grow up as distinct individuals, yet our spiritual roots are interlaced with our Father in Heaven and all His children. Together we should "stand fast in one spirit, with one mind striving together for the faith of the gospel" (Philippians 1:27). These entwining aspens also symbolize how the members of the Godhead can be three distinct beings while maintaining a wholly merged oneness of purpose.

Unique Unity as Separate Individuals

God the Father, Jesus Christ, and the Holy Ghost possess a unique unity. They do not inhabit the same body, but are individual beings. The Holy Ghost is an entity of spirit, while the Father and the Son have "flesh and bones as tangible as man's" (D&C 130:22). Because the Godhead remains forever one in thought, they behave exactly alike.

New Testament references to the oneness of the Father, Son, and Holy Spirit have caused many Christians to falsely believe in a trinity. It's a mystery to me how people can believe that these three members of the Godhead can be one in substance, yet with three separate personas. Through the restored gospel of Jesus Christ, Latter-day Saints understand that the trinity is a deception Satan uses to divide religious faiths rather than unify their doctrines. In contrast, Jesus wants to gather all God's children together so there will be "one fold, and one shepherd" (John 10:16).

From an eternal perspective, our Father desires that all of us become like Him—unified in words, thoughts, faith, love, and actions. Not every son on earth can completely duplicate his father, nor can each daughter fully replicate her mother. In the same light, our Father in Heaven does not expect His children to look precisely like Him or His Beloved Son. Yet there must be some resemblance, in form and in spirit, as President Joseph F. Smith explained, "We are God's children, and therefore must resemble his Son in person, and also spiritually, so far as we will obey the principles of the gospel of eternal truth. For, we were foreordained ... to become conformed to his likeness through the wise and proper use of our free agency" (*Gospel Doctrine*, 57–58).

How is it that you and I can be "born of God" and receive "his image in [our] countenance" (Alma 5:14)? Will we need plastic surgery? Face lifts? Botox treatments? Of course not, though the older I get, the more I consider such things. The most important aspect of oneness is not our outer appearance, but our inner resemblance to God.

Each and every person on earth is cherished by the Father, Son, and Holy Ghost. That means you! There are no exceptions. Our safety, salvation, and eventual exaltation continually occupies the minds of each member of the Godhead.

Hearts Knit Together In Unity

Visualize countless strands of multicolored yarn knitted together to form one whole. I don't mean a disorganized blob of yarn, as a pair of playful kittens might make—but something created in an organized and well-thought-out fashion. At the waters of Mormon, Alma instructed his people to have "their hearts knit together in unity and in love one towards another" (Mosiah 18:21). In addition, He "commanded them that there should be no contention one with another, but that they should look forward with one eye, having one faith and one baptism" (v. 21).

The Apostle Paul also advised that people's "hearts may be comforted, being knit together in love," (Colossians 2:2). Knitting is a way to interweave yarn into comforting clothes or blankets that provide warmth. If our lives are woven together with spiritual fiber, the heartfelt knitted fabric can soothe cruelties and cover coldness that humans sometimes inflict upon each other.

Remember the commandment, "Love thy neighbor as thyself," which is repeated in Leviticus, Matthew, Mark, Luke, Romans, Galatians, James, Third Nephi, and the Doctrine and Covenants. Clearly, the Lord meant what He said, "Love one another, as I have loved you" (John 15:12). I think He still means it. Profound, pure love is the prominent character trait we must possess to be awarded permanent residency in the kingdom of God.

Conclusion

In ancient times, Paul taught of oneness as a community: "That ye may with one mind and one mouth glorify God, even the Father of our Lord Jesus Christ. Wherefore receive ye one another, as Christ also received us to the glory of God" (Romans 15: 6-7). In these latter days, our Father has requested that "every man esteem his brother as himself,... I say unto you, be one; and *if ye are not one ye are not mine*" (D&C 38:24, 27, italics added).

Do you remember how Kermit the Frog sang, "It's not easy being green." Well, it's also not easy being "one." It might take some blood-letting—akin to having a phlebotomist draw blood for medical tests—for us to pass celestial tests of worthiness. But because Jesus accepted the Father's will and shed His innocent blood for us, it behooves us to follow His example. Eternal life and exaltation await us if we do all that is required.

Jesus taught "the Father and I are One. I am in the Father and the Father in me; and inasmuch as ye have received me, ye are in me and I in you" (D&C 50:43). Those who achieve oneness with Christ will be awarded oneness with the Father. One significant reason Christ came to earth was to help us better comprehend our Father in Heaven, as Elder Jeffrey R. Holland explained:

Of the many magnificent purposes served in the life and ministry of the Lord Jesus Christ, one great aspect of that mission often goes uncelebrated.... It is the grand truth that in all that Jesus came to say and do, including and especially in His atoning suffering and sacrifice, He was showing us who and what God our Eternal Father is like, how completely devoted He is to His children in every age and nation. In word and in deed Jesus was trying to reveal and make personal to us the true nature of His Father, our Father in Heaven....

To come to earth with such a responsibility, to stand in place of Elohim—speaking as He would speak, judging and serving, loving and warning, forbearing and forgiving as He would do—this is a duty of such staggering proportions that you and I cannot comprehend such a thing. But in the loyalty and determination that would be characteristic of a divine child, Jesus could comprehend it and He did it. Then, when the praise and honor began to come, He humbly directed all adulation to the Father. ["The Grandeur of God," *Ensign*, November 2003, 70–71.]

How blessed will you and I be when we fully comprehend the magnificence of our Father and learn to represent Him, as did Jesus, with perfect honor and loyalty. Our only way to reach the Father is through His Beloved Son. Nothing we do in and of ourselves is worthwhile without Christ's infinite and eternal sacrifice.

His mission—the Atonement—was uniquely His. Only one was required to do that. He did it once for all [God's children]. On the other hand, His ministry was to be an example for us. There is no limit to the number of people who can learn to love as He loved, to serve, obey, pray, and endure to the end as He did. We can all emulate that example. [Russell M. Nelson, "The Mission and Ministry of the Savior," *Ensign*, June 2005, 19.]

Though it may often seem beyond our earthly ability, I believe we can learn to emulate Christ's example, become one with Him, and thus be eternally united with our Father. May this earnest goal become yours and mine—daily, hourly, and minute by minute.

For additional insight see:

Lorenzo Snow, "Blessings of the Gospel Only Obtained by Compliance to the Law," *Ensign*, Oct. 1971, 16–22.

Neal A. Maxwell, *Of One Heart*, Deseret Book Co., Salt Lake City, 1975.

That in the dispensation of the fulness of times
he might gather together in one all things in Christ,
both which are in heaven,
and which are on the earth, even in him.
Ephesians 1:10

Fullness

Can you picture the day when everything and everyone are gathered together as one in Christ? It's prophesied "that in the dispensation of the fulness of times God might gather together in one all things in Christ, both which are in heaven, and which are on the earth, even in him" (Ephesians 1:10). This unique dispensation of fulness began with the restoration of the gospel through the Prophet Joseph Smith, who wrote the following:

It is necessary in the ushering in of the dispensation of the fulness of times, *which dispensation is now beginning to usher in*, that a whole and complete and perfect union, and welding together of dispensations, and keys, and powers, and glories should take place, and be revealed from the days of Adam even to the present time. And not only this, but those things which never have been revealed from the foundation of the world, but have been kept hid from the wise and prudent, shall be revealed unto babes and sucklings in this, the dispensation of the fulness of times.

Now, what do we hear in the gospel which we have received? A voice of gladness! A voice of mercy from heaven; and a voice of truth out of the earth; glad tidings for the dead; a voice of gladness for the living and the dead; glad tidings of great joy. [D&C 128:18–19, italics added.]

Gladness, mercy, truth, and joy! What a blessed, fulfilling time is the dispensation of the fulness of times! For those of you who crave three square meals daily, "fulness of times" has nothing to do with your stomach. Rather it is spiritual completeness—a wholeness and oneness—a "fulness of the gospel of the Messiah" (1 Nephi 15:13). What the Father desires for His children is not just an ordinary life, but an abundant life (see John 10:10), not merely peace, but "the peace of God, which passeth all understanding" (Philippians 4:7). Eventually, fulness means that "all [the] Father hath shall be given" to those who are worthy (D&C 84:38).

In our latter-day scriptures, "fulness" is connected to other words of eternal significance: fulness of glory (D&C 132:6), fulness of truth (D&C 93:26), and fulness of joy (D&C 138:17).

A Fulness of Joy

Joy in our earthly lives is connected with the Holy Ghost and with faith in Christ, as shown by King Benjamin's people: "The Spirit of the Lord came upon them, and they were filled with joy, … because of the exceeding faith which they had in Jesus Christ" (Mosiah 4:3). Earthly pleasures bring temporary happiness, but deep joy is possible only through the Spirit. "I will impart unto you of my Spirit, which shall enlighten your mind, which shall fill your soul with joy" (D&C 11:13).

Eternal joy is exhibited by those in the spirit world, as revealed to President Joseph F. Smith. "All these had departed the mortal life, firm in the hope of a glorious resurrection,… I beheld that they were filled with joy and gladness, and were rejoicing together" (D&C 138:14–15). Enoch also witnessed joy through redemption: "And the Lord showed Enoch all things, even unto the end of the world, and he saw the day of the righteous, the hour of their redemption, and received a fulness of joy" (Moses 7:67). True and everlasting joy is possible only after our bodies and spirits are reunited. We can't celebrate by clapping our hands and giving each other high-fives until we obtain a resurrected state. Hugs will be difficult to give and receive without the body's reconnection to the spirit. Body slams will also be impossible.

> For man is spirit. The elements [of the body] are eternal, and spirit and element inseparably connected, receive a fulness of joy;
> And when separated, man cannot receive a fulness of joy (D&C 93:33–34).
> Wherefore, fear not even unto death; for in this world your joy is not full, but in me your joy is full (D&C 101:36).

Through Christ's atonement and resurrection, we can obtain everlasting joy, even if adversity plagued our earthly lives. During His mortal life in Palestine, the Lord's life was fraught with trials and sorrows over the wickedness of His people. But after His resurrection, while visiting the Nephites, Jesus acknowledged a fulness of joy: "And they arose from the earth, and he said unto them: Blessed are ye because of your faith. And now behold, my joy is full" (3 Nephi 17:20). He later explained that eternal joy is a gift from our Father: "Ye shall have fulness of joy;... your joy shall be full, even as the Father hath given me fulness of joy, and ye shall be even as I am" (3 Nephi 28:10). Eternal life is the greatest gift God the Father bestows upon His children (see D&C 14:7). Thus, it is filled with tremendous joy.

When my father died in 1992, my youngest son was thirteen and curious about life and death. One day he asked with a hint of humor, "Do you think they celebrate 'death days' in heaven like we celebrate birthdays on earth?"

"Of course!" I replied. "But rather than brief celebrations like birthday parties, the rejoicing goes on throughout eternity."

Fantastic festivities and feasts forever! Then "will the Lord of Hosts make unto all people a feast of fat things, a feast of wines on the lees" (Isaiah 25:6). Everyone is invited—even people who were once "strangers and foreigners" can be "fellowcitizens with the Saints, and of the household of God" (Ephesians 2:19). No RSVP is necessary. Just repent and follow Christ, who said, "Come unto me, ye blessed, there is a place prepared for you in the mansions of my Father" (Enos 1:27). And if, in the midst of our celebrations, we run out of "wine on the lees," well, don't worry; Jesus once fixed that same problem at a wedding in Cana.

Christ's message of joy in redemption should be shouted from housetops, proclaimed from hot air balloons, and streamed across the sky by orbiting satellites. Though occasionally people try to change the message of truth, instead, the message should change people. The gospel of Jesus Christ is of inestimable, everlasting value—because our Savior paid an infinite price for our salvation.

Receiving a Fulness

Before the world was formed, Jesus prepared to advance as the Son of God. Though divinely endowed, He had to learn "precept upon precept, line upon line" (Isaiah 28:10–13), just as we must do. Notice the repetition in the scriptures below, explaining that Christ gradually ascended toward the Father's fulness:

> And I, John, saw that he received not of the fulness at the first, but received grace for grace;
> And he received not of the fulness at first, but continued from grace to grace, until he received a fulness;
> And thus he was called the Son of God, because he received not of the fulness at the first.
> And I, John, bear record that he received a fulness of the glory of the Father;
> And he received all power, both in heaven and on earth, and the glory of the Father was with him, for he dwelt in him (D&C 93:12–14, 16–17).

Though Jesus "received not of the fulness at first," eventually He did gain the power, glory, and fulness of the Father. Each of us can advance in a similar manner if we patiently persevere—during this life and the next.

Finding and staying true to our faith in God may be more of a struggle for some than for others. For example, I present my second grandson. At the tender age of five, he tapped his mother's arm and looked up at her with a ponderous expression on his face. Their family had been living in Hong Kong for a year, and at that moment they were seated in sacrament meeting. "Mom," he said rather astutely for his age, "I think the story of Jesus is fiction."

This little boy often used a prodigious vocabulary, but that particular statement provoked worry in both his parents. As weeks went by, he continued to make edgy comments that questioned the existence of God. One day in Primary, his mother taught the sharing time lesson, then she closed her words by saying, "I know God lives, and—." Before she could finish, her son interrupted, "But, Mom, I don't know that!" Even the prayers of this five-year-old reflected the dilemma in his young mind.

Needless to say, at their Family Home Evenings and other family discussions, these dutiful parents often bore testimony of Heavenly Father and Jesus Christ. For a time, they wondered if moving to Hong Kong for an employment opportunity had been the best choice for the spiritual upbringing of their five children.

After several months of gentle instruction from his parents, this boy gradually received answers to his questions. Then his prayers reflected more faith and understanding, as, precept upon precept and line upon line, he gained confidence that God was real. By July, when their family came to stay with us in Salt Lake City, we were grateful to see our grandson's testimony of the Father and Son had stabilized. Now he can forge ahead in studying the gospel, though I suspect his inquiring mind may need answers to other doctrinal questions in the future.

Many people question the validity of scriptures and the reality of God, though usually not at the age of five. At any stage of life when faith wavers, it doesn't help to turn away from the gospel, but rather we must delve more deeply into it to enhance our enlightenment.

We must not allow ourselves to be discouraged whenever we discover our weakness. We can scarcely find an instance in all the glorious examples set us by the prophets, ancient or modern, wherein they permitted the Evil One to discourage them; but on the other hand they constantly sought to overcome, to win the prize, and thus prepare themselves for a fulness of glory. [Lorenzo Snow, "Blessings of the Gospel Only Obtained by Compliance to the Law," reprinted in *Ensign*, Oct. 1971, 21.]

A tulip doesn't sprout from a bulb and bloom in one day. Similarly, receiving a fulness of glory is a gradual process which requires faith in Christ and a determination to keep the commandments. The Lord has promised, "that you may come unto the Father in my name, and in due time receive of his fulness. For if you keep my commandments you shall receive of his fulness, and be glorified in me as I am in the Father; therefore, I say unto you, you shall receive grace for grace…. And no man receiveth a fulness unless he keepeth his commandments (D&C 93:19, 20, 27).

Rely on the Prophets

Just as my grandson was taught through his parents' testimonies, we all can benefit from reliance on testimonies of the prophets—from ancient or latter days. During my college years at Utah State University, President Harold B. Lee spoke at a student fireside. I still recall how President Lee attested to the truthfulness of the gospel and gave witness of the reality of Christ's mission. Then he proposed that those in the audience who didn't yet have a personal witness of the truth could lean on his testimony while they developed their own.

And therefore, he that will harden his heart, the same receiveth the lesser portion of the word; and he that will not harden his heart, to him is given the greater portion of the word, until it is given unto him to know the mysteries of God until he know them in full (Alma 12:10).

How about that? We can know the mysteries of God in their fulness! I suppose that will take more than a little asking, seeking, and knocking. "Ask, and it shall be given you; seek, and ye shall find; knock, and the door shall be opened unto you" (Luke 10:9).

Jesus Christ is always available. You don't have to schedule an appointment to knock on His door. He is always with you, whether you realize it or not. Of course, just because He's always with you doesn't mean you can drive in the car pool lane on the freeway. Then you'd soon have a cop with you, too. That reminds me, Jesus will never ask to see your identification. He knows you thoroughly—much better than you know yourself. Therefore, it's vital to heed His counsel so you can progress and become everything the Father created you to be.

The Process of Progression

Though tutored directly by Jesus Christ, the chief apostle, Simon Peter, endured numerous stretching experiences to overcome his human frailties and rise to God's expectations of him. Like all mortals, including prophets and apostles, he had weaknesses and strengths which either thwarted or enhanced his spirituality (see "Peter," LDS Bible Dictionary, 749).

At their first encounter, Jesus said to him, "Thou art Simon the son of Jona: thou shalt be called Cephas, which is by interpretation, A stone" (John 1:42). Though Jesus acknowledged the rock-like tenacity of Peter, He undoubtedly saw the need to polish and smooth the rough edges of this durable disciple.

Peter already knew how to work long hours as a fisherman, often toiling through the night to earn his hire. After one such laborious, yet unfruitful, night, Peter and his partners wearily returned to shore to mend their nets. Then into their midst came Jesus—though He was not alone, for a throng of people, longing to hear the word of God, pressed upon Him. Jesus found a place to sit in Simon Peter's ship on the shore, from where He could teach. Later, as the crowd dispersed, Jesus suggested that the fishermen launch out once again and let down their nets.

And Simon answering said unto him, Master, we have toiled all the night, and have taken nothing: nevertheless at thy word I will let down the net.

And when they had this done, they inclosed a great multitude of fishes: and their net brake.

And they beckoned unto their partners, which were in the other ship, that they should come and help them. And they came, and filled both the ships, so that they began to sink.

When Simon Peter saw it, he fell down at Jesus' knees, saying, Depart from me; for I am a sinful man, O Lord (Luke 5:5–8).

Peter had enough faith to heed the Lord's counsel to again sail out and put down the nets. He instantly recognized, by the resulting overflow of fish, that this miracle was from God. Then, as many of us might react, Peter called himself a sinful man, unworthy to be near Christ. Yet, "Jesus said unto Simon, Fear not; from henceforth thou shalt catch men" (v. 11). So Peter and his brother Andrew "straightway left their nets, and followed him" (v. 20). Straightway, immediately, without question or hesitation.

For some people, it might be difficult to leave fishing behind. My husband would probably have had to think about it. But not me. I've never been a fan of fishing—especially when it comes to cleaning and gutting them at the end of the day. Maybe Peter and Andrew were tired of cleaning fish, so they eagerly followed Jesus and became "fishers of men" (Matthew 4:19). Perhaps Jesus said, you "catch men," and I'll clean them. Sounds like a fine deal to me. Isn't that what Christ does? He cleanses and purifies men and women through the power of His Atonement.

Follow Christ

Those who followed Christ through Palestine personally witnessed His many miracles: "healing all manner of sickness" (Matthew 4:23), feeding the five thousand with a few loaves and fishes (Matthew 14:15–21), calming storms upon the Sea of Galilee (Matthew 8 and 14), and so on. Many felt the fire of testimony burn within their hearts when Jesus spoke His Sermon on the Mount: "whosoever shall smite thee on they right cheek, turn to him the other also…. Love your enemies, bless them that curse you, do good to them that hate you, and pray for them which despitefully use you and persecute you" (Matthew 5:39, 44). However, most people did not fully comprehend who Jesus was. They questioned His divinity as the Son of God, especially the day He taught that He is the bread of life (see John 6).

> From that time many of his disciples went back, and walked no more with him.
> Then said Jesus unto the twelve, Will ye also go away?
> Then Simon Peter answered him, Lord, to whom shall we go? Thou hast the words of eternal life.
> And we believe and are sure that thou art that Christ, the Son of the living God (John 6:66–69).

Though Peter rendered this mighty testimony, he was still vulnerable to doubt and fear. Sometimes he spoke his mind, allowing his human frailties to show through in his willful personality. Like many of us, he tried to put a question mark where Jesus had put a period. One day, Jesus reprimanded Peter:

> Get thee behind me, Satan: for thou savorest not the things that be of God, but the things that be of men….
> Whosoever will come after me, let him deny himself, and take up his cross, and follow me.
> For whosoever will save his life shall lose it; but whosoever shall lose his life for my sake and the gospel's, the same shall save it (Mark 8:31–35).

Even with this admonition, Peter wavered from time to time, as most people do. He went through peaks and valleys—no doubt recognizing his need to repent and return to the straight and narrow path. Though cautioned to not revile against his enemies, Peter forgot to "turn the other cheek" (Matthew 5:39). During the sudden crisis when soldiers came to arrest Jesus at the garden of Gethsemane, Peter "having a sword drew it, and smote the high priest's servant, and cut off his right ear" (John 18:10).

With compassion for the wounded servant, Jesus "touched his ear, and healed him" (Luke 22:51). Perhaps Peter chided himself, saying, "What a mistake that was! Perhaps I'm not worthy to be an apostle. Will I get fired?" Undoubtedly his heart still stung with the warning Jesus had given him an hour before: "Verily I say unto thee, That this day, even in this night, before the cock crow twice, thou shalt deny me thrice" (Mark 14:30).

Peter kept a safe distance behind the band of men who took Jesus to an arraignment before the Jewish leaders. While waiting in the courtyard with strangers, Peter was accused three times of being an associate to Christ. Three times he denied it. Then "the Lord turned, and looked upon Peter. And Peter remembered the word of the Lord, how he had said unto him, Before the cock crow, thou shalt deny me thrice" (Luke 22:61). What a pivotal, poignant moment! Peter knew he'd denied the Lord, then he had to look into His Master's face! No wonder "Peter went out, and wept bitterly" (v. 62).

Perhaps those tears were the decisive turning point for Peter. I suspect he spent the next three days in introspection—all the while Jesus endured the mock trials, crucifixion, and entombment. No doubt Peter deeply grieved and mourned for the loss of his Master. When finally, after Christ's resurrection, women offered reports of the empty tomb, Peter rebounded with wholehearted enthusiasm, "and ran unto the sepulchre; and stooping down, he beheld the linen clothes laid by themselves, and departed, *wondering in himself* at that which was come to pass" (Luke 24:12, italics added).

Wondering in himself. Is it possible that during his years at the Savior's side, Peter never had to wonder in himself? Maybe he had never been forced to stand alone on his conviction of Christ's divinity as the Son of God. Perhaps that's why Jesus had admonished him, "when thou art converted, strengthen thy brethren" (Luke 22:32).

On the shore of Galilee, after the resurrection, the risen Lord once again communed with the Chief Apostle. After asking three times if Peter loved Him, Jesus admonished, "Feed my sheep. Feed my lambs" (John 21:15–17). From that time forward, Peter never wavered in his testimony of Christ. Rather, he diligently exhorted his brethren to "feed the flock of God which is among you" (1 Peter 5:2).

Peter's acceleration toward a fulness of knowledge and testimony of Christ was neither swift nor steady. That gives me hope. My own spirituality has not been a straight line toward "fulness," but rather, my progress is both sporadic and erratic. Yet I know if we live "by every word which proceedeth forth out of the mouth of God," He "will give unto the faithful line upon line, precept upon precept; and [he] will try you and prove you herewith" (D&C 98:11–12). Only then will you and I be prepared to receive the fulness of the Father.

In the Beginning

Just as Jesus was present with God before the world was made, we also existed as intelligences (see D&C 93:7, 29). Though we did not have equal enlightenment with God and Christ, They saw our potential to improve and become like Them. "And the Lord said unto me: These two facts do exist, that there are two spirits, one being more intelligent than the other; there shall be another more intelligent than they; I am the Lord thy God, I am more intelligent than they all" (Abraham 3:19). The Prophet Joseph Smith added the following: "God himself, finding he was in the midst of spirits and glory, because he was more intelligent, saw proper to institute laws whereby the rest could have a privilege to advance like himself." [Joseph Smith, *History of the Church*, 6:312.]

How selfless and magnanimous of our Father to desire that all His children have a chance to progress toward the standing at which He had arrived! Each of us shouted for joy at the opportunity to come to earth (see Job 38:7). Yet how many of us shout for joy as we go about our day-to-day lives? Perhaps, like me, you await rejoicing in the celestial kingdom. But we have every reason to be joyful now! Despite our mortal imperfections, the day will come those "who are quickened by a portion of the celestial glory shall then receive of the same, even a fulness" (D&C 88:29).

Ever wonder what "quickening" might feel like? It has nothing to do with getting out of quicksand. It's more like being speedy and quick like the animated Road Runner who says "Beep, beep!" and races away from Wile E. Coyote. Quicken means to enliven, animate, energize, revitalize, activate, or accelerate. A spiritual quickening is to revive the soul—the body and spirit—into a state of glory. My sense is that quickening can partially occur on earth, and later the process will be completed in eternal realms ahead.

Each of us starts in a minuscule manner, like a seed that sprouts and grows out of the dark soil into the light. Only then can the plant begin its stretch heavenward—and that doesn't happen overnight like Jack's magic beanstalk that instantly reached the clouds. In a similar manner, humans slowly progress from tiny embryos to babies, then toddlers, children, teenagers, and later adults. Adulthood also comes in many stages, some of which we don't like to admit, such as middle age—when our age starts to show around our middle. Our final advancement, if we prove worthy, will be evolving into a god or goddess.

> Man is the child of God, formed in the divine image and endowed with divine attributes, and even as the infant son of an earthly father and mother is capable in due time of becoming a man, so the undeveloped offspring of celestial parentage is capable, by experience through ages and [eons], of evolving into a God. [Joseph F. Smith, *The Origin of Man by the First Presidency of the Church*, 81.]

It's intimidating to envision myself receiving a fulness of glory, since I'm merely one tiny entity amid the vast sprawl of the universe. Yet I'm comforted to know that God sees my potential, and He also understands the difficult and frequent detours I often must take around worldly distractions in order to focus on matters of eternal significance. Our spiritual journeys can seem like "Mission Impossible." But then, movies and television aren't reality. The truth is that our spirits are divinely conceived, and we are capable of attaining a holy and supreme level of perfection. Remember that our Father in Heaven began in a similar manner to His children.

> God himself was once as we are now, and is an exalted man, and sits enthroned in yonder heavens! That is the great secret. If the veil were rent today,... you would see him like a man in form—like yourselves in all the person, image, and very form as a man; for Adam was created in the very fashion, image, and likeness of God, and received instruction from, and walked, talked and conversed with Him, as one man talks and communes with another.... It is the first principle of the gospel to know for a certainty the character of God, and to know that we may converse with him as one man converses with another, and that He was once a man like us; yea, that God himself, the Father of us all, dwelt on an earth, the same as Jesus Christ Himself did. [Joseph Smith, *History of the Church*, 6:305.]

Realizing that our Father dwelt on an earth may bring to mind what President Lorenzo Snow wrote in 1840: "The Spirit of the Lord rested mightily upon me—the eyes of my understanding were opened, and I saw as clear as the sun at noonday, with wonder and astonishment, the pathway of God and man, I formed the following couplet which expresses the revelation as it was shown me.... As man now is, God once was: As God now is, man may be."

Conclusion

Our goal to become "as God now is" should keep our minds and hearts centered on matters of eternal importance. It's amazing to think that every inhabitant on the earth has the potential to become gods and goddesses. That should improve our interaction with those around us, as theologian C. S. Lewis said in a sermon called "The Weight of Glory."

The load, or weight, or burden of my neighbor's glory should be laid daily on my back, a load so heavy that only humility can carry it, and the backs of the proud will be broken. It is a serious thing to live in a society of possible gods and goddesses, to remember that the dullest and most uninteresting person you can talk to may one day be a creature which, if you saw it now, you would be strongly tempted to worship.... It is in light of these overwhelming possibilities, it is with the awe and circumspection proper to them, that we should conduct all our dealings with one another, all friendships, all loves, all play, all politics. There are no ordinary people. You have never talked to a mere mortal. Nations, cultures, arts, civilizations—these are mortal, and their life is to ours as the life of a gnat. But it is immortals whom we joke with, work with, marry, snub, and exploit.... [Yet] your neighbor is the holiest object presented to your senses.

God will not be mad at us if we treat each other with the respect due to potential gods and goddesses. Nor will He be disappointed if we always remember His Son, Jesus Christ, and strive to become like Him. I know He will bless us for each noble, humble, and dedicated effort we make. Our destination is far beyond earthly civilization, for we seek eternal celestialization.

Although receiving fulness of the Father's glory cannot occur until the next life—it should be our prime goal on earth. Our Savior has promised, "For if you keep my commandments you shall receive of his fulness, and be glorified in me as I am in the Father; therefore, I say unto you, you shall receive grace for grace" (D&C 93:20).

For additional insight see:
Joseph F. Smith, "The Origin of Man by the First Presidency of the Church."
Gary J. Coleman, "Watchmen of the Lord," *Ensign*, Sept. 2006, 64–67.

And of his fulness have all received,
and grace for grace.
John 1:16

Grace for Grace

Jesus offered fulness to the Twelve Apostles, as John witnessed: "And of his fulness have all we received, and grace for grace" (John 1:16). The phrase *grace for grace* implies that Christ provided a blessing of grace after the apostles' acts of righteous grace. Grace is a reciprocal principle—for apostles and prophets as well as the rest of us.

Though teachings of grace abound in the New Testament, it has caused some debate among Christian sects. Is grace a free gift from God, or is work required to receive it? "For by grace are ye saved through faith; and that not of yourselves: it is the gift of God: Not of works, lest any man boast" (Ephesians 2:8–9). The Book of Mormon clarifies grace: "And may God grant, in his great fulness, that men might be brought unto repentance and good works, that they might be restored unto grace for grace, according to their works" (Helaman 12:24). Balance is found in combining our righteous works with the divine gift of empowering grace.

If you stand idly beside the track that leads to the state of grace, the train will pass you by. First you must pay the price for a ticket, which requires diligent effort. Then, of course, there are those who try to do too much—endeavoring to save themselves without relying on Christ's Atonement. They stand, confident and self-assured, directly on the track to grace. Then they get run over, because of their lack of understanding of what grace truly is.

Grace is a gift from God, which people can receive after they have exerted all their strength and energy to reach eternal life. Only our Savior's atonement can intercede to replace any human frailties and imperfections that remain from life on earth. Divine grace sufficiently fills in the gap which divides a person from exaltation. Yet it takes effect only after that individual has done everything to obtain the goal. No one—no matter how righteous and repentant—is capable of achieving eternal life without the gift of grace.

Great and Marvelous Work

Each child of God is offered grace through Christ's mercy, love, and selfless sacrifice, but only in proportion to their faithfulness. "For we labor diligently to write, to persuade our children, and also our brethren, to believe in Christ, and to be reconciled to God; for we know that it is by grace we are saved, after all we can do" (2 Nephi 25:23). *All we can do* requires extensive endeavors beyond keeping the commandments and avoiding evil. It means wholehearted consecration to building the kingdom of God. But don't get discouraged while enduring to the end. God won't judge us until after we're dead. Neither should we judge others until after we're dead.

Jesus set an example, saying, "I must work the works of him that sent me while it is day: the night cometh, when no man can work" (John 9:4). It's never too late to begin steady employment as a servant of God, for "this life is the time for men to prepare to meet God, yea, behold the day of this life is the day for men to perform their labors" (Alma 34:32).

Righteous labors are more than quick preparations for Sundays, as we sang in Primary: "We clean the house, and we shop at the store,/ So we won't have to work until Monday. We brush our clothes, and we shine our shoes,/... So we can be ready for Sunday!" ["Saturday," *Children's Songbook*, 196.]

Living the gospel is not merely a Sunday-go-to-church enterprise. Rather, it's a daily pursuit of righteousness that will spiritually edify ourselves, our loved ones, and all within our reach. We are "instruments in [God's] hands of doing this *great and marvelous work*" (Alma 26:15, italics added). Is building the kingdom of God a great work? Oh, yes! And is it a marvelous work? Absolutely!

Remember that grace is a reciprocal principle. When you and I are "strong in the grace that is in Christ Jesus" (2 Timothy 2:1), we can achieve eternal grace and exaltation through the Lord's atonement.

Receiving Grace for Grace

From time to time, I have been guilty of not climbing toward the celestial kingdom. I get weary and remain on a plateau, or slide slightly downhill. But that's contrary to our eternal progress, which Satan endeavors to thwart. Although we can't expect life's journey to be effortless and painless, it's through overcoming adversity and increasing righteousness that we strengthen our spiritual muscles enough to ascend unto heaven.

For decades, scientists have studied the curious life cycle of coral reefs. These small organisms often grow in environments where harsh ocean currents thrash their communities. Compared to coral found in placid waters, the colonies in hostile areas are much more sturdy and productive. Most humans also become hardier and heartier through facing trials. While Abraham lived among the Egyptians, he narrowly escaped being sacrificed on their idolatrous altar. But rather than fearing their evil ways, his faith in God and zeal for righteousness increased. Abraham cried unto the Lord, who spared his life, and later proclaimed great spiritual gifts upon him, including the priesthood lineage.

And finding there was greater happiness and peace and rest for me, I sought for the blessings of the fathers [priesthood], and the right [authority] whereunto I should be ordained to administer the same; having been myself a follower of righteousness, desiring also to be one who possessed great knowledge, and to be a greater follower of righteousness, and to possess a greater knowledge, and to be a father of many nations, a prince of peace, and desiring to receive instructions, and to keep the commandments of God, I became a rightful heir, a High Priest, holding the right belonging to the fathers (Abraham 1:2).

For each advancement Abraham made in righteousness, God blessed him with increased knowledge. This is what is meant by receiving grace for grace. Like Abraham, the more we increase our faith and works, the more our Father blesses us with knowledge and power to serve Him.

Lengthen Your Stride

Latter-day Saints will recognize the phrase "lengthen your stride" as one used repeatedly by President Spencer W. Kimball. Other motivational phrases for which He was known are "broaden your vision" and "do it now!" In a meeting to inspire mission presidents, he added other memorable phrases, "Put your shoulders to the wheel, lengthen your stride, heighten your reach, increase your devotion and that of the missionaries so that we can begin to move the work along more rapidly." [*The Teachings of Spencer W. Kimball,* 564.]

Most people begin with baby steps, not giant leaps, in learning to apply gospel truths. "Behold, ye are little children and ye cannot bear all things now; ye must grow in grace and in the knowledge of the truth" (D&C 50:40). On the pathway to eternity, there should be no fretting if your momentum slows down occasionally—that's what repentance is for. Don't worry if your shoelaces get tangled and you trip over your own feet. Also, avoid any stumbling blocks Satan tosses into your pathway. Just persevere and continue a steady pursuit toward increased spirituality—day after day and night after night, as the classic poem by Henry Wadsworth Longfellow states:

> The heights by great men, reached and kept, were not obtained by sudden flight,
> But they, while their companions slept, were toiling upwards in the night.

Whether day or night, our Father in Heaven provides wisdom and strength in exchange for our prayers. "And if men come unto me I will show unto them their weakness. I give unto men weakness that they may be humble; and *my grace is sufficient* for all men that humble themselves before me; for if they humble themselves before me, and have faith in me, then will I make weak things become strong unto them" (Ether 12:27, italics added). If weakness overcomes you from time to time, remember that the Prophet Moses began life as a basket case.

God's grace takes effect after you and I expend effort to receive it. It takes determination and courage to overcome our weaknesses of the flesh. Unlike the cowardly lion, we won't need to ask the emperor of Oz to give us courage. Nor will we have to heroically shrink the Wicked Witch of the West by dousing her with water— though we may have to quench some "fiery darts of the adversary" (D&C 3:8).

It doesn't matter what anyone else may judge our progress to be, because our Father in Heaven sets a different pace for each of His children. He doesn't think the same way as you and me—thank goodness! Otherwise, He might not have offered us the potential to become gods and goddesses. "For my thoughts are not your thoughts, nor are my ways your ways, saith the Lord. For as the heavens are higher than the earth, so are my ways higher than your ways, and my thoughts higher than your thoughts" (Isaiah 55:8–9).

Because of His exalted perspective, God the Father can discern our eternal possibilities, even when we are clueless. It should cheer us up to realize His confidence in you and me.

Therefore, cheer up your hearts, and remember that ye are free to act for yourselves—to choose the way of everlasting death or the way of eternal life.

Wherefore, my beloved brethren, reconcile yourselves to the will of God,... [for] it is only in and through the grace of God that ye are saved.

Wherefore, may God raise you from death by the power of the resurrection, and also from everlasting death by the power of the atonement, that ye may be received into the eternal kingdom of God, that ye may praise him through grace divine (2 Nephi 10:23–25).

Despite weaknesses of the flesh, our spirits are endowed with divine qualities that can gradually mature and blossom. The grace of God is offered freely to all those who humbly repent and reach out to grasp the proffered gift of the atonement. "Every one of us is given grace according to the measure of the gift of Christ" (Ephesians. 4:7).

Seed of Deity

Because we are "begotten sons and daughters unto God" (D&C 76:24), the seeds of godliness are planted within us. It may require deep introspection to uncover the spiritual giant that resides within us.

During a visit to Sequoia National Park in California, I learned why those gigantic trees can grow as large as forty feet in diameter and up to 300 feet tall. Within the sequoia is tannin, or tannic acid, which helps in resisting insects, fire, and disease. This resilience helps the sequoias live to be so ancient and enormous. I like to compare tannin in the sequoia to the Spirit of the Lord within me. When I heed the Spirit's voice, I'm better able to resist temptation and overcome the cares of the world.

Despite the lofty size of sequoias, their pinecones are relatively small, similar to a normal egg. It takes two years for the sequoia cones to fully develop, then they can remain on the trees for as long as 20 years. Each small cone contains two or three hundred seeds—each the size of an oat flake. These small but fruitful seeds are usually released from the cones by the intense heat of wildfires. About one in six hundred thousand seeds will successfully sprout— only if the soil is mineral-rich, and the forest provides enough nurturing sunlight and water. The sprout begins as an inch-long tap root, which later sends a shoot upward. It takes hundreds of years for that tiny plant to become a full-grown sequoia.

I keep a sequoia cone on my desk to remind me of the seeds of godliness within me. Like these massive trees, I can evolve into a spiritual giant if I endure life with steadfast faith in Jesus Christ. May it be that "he, through his infinite goodness and grace will keep you through the endurance of faith on his name to the end" (Moroni 8:3).

I Will Go and Do

When we more fully understand matters of eternity, we show more courage in our earthly lives, as did Nephi, who said, "I will go and do the things which the Lord hath commanded, for I know that the Lord giveth no commandments unto the children of men, save he shall prepare a way for them to accomplish the thing which he commandeth them" (1 Nephi 3:7). That was when Lehi asked his sons to return to Jerusalem to get the brass plates from Laban. Their journey was harsh. I've seen portions of the wilderness through which they traveled: dry, bleak, water-less. But Nephi and his brothers agreed to journey back through the dusty desert and, with faith in divine assistance, they accomplished their task.

Nephi also showed transcendent courage when faced with building a ship. Since he was a "city boy" from Jerusalem, it's likely he'd never been to the seashore nor seen a ship large enough to carry his family and their provisions across the ocean. Yet he offers this profound message of faith that remains true for righteous individuals in today's world:

If God had commanded me to do all things I could do them. If he should command me that I should say unto this water, be thou earth, it should be earth; and if I should say it, it would be done.

And now, if the Lord has such great power, and has wrought so many miracles among the children of men, how is it that he cannot instruct me, that I should build a ship? [1 Nephi 17:50–51]

What better way to subdue human fears and frailties than to trust the Lord to prepare the way? I admire Nephi's faith and tenacity. "Courage is resistance to fear, mastery of fear—not absence of fear" (Mark Twain). When fears and inadequacies are vanquished through faith in God, we're better able to bless the lives of others.

Remember the turnaround of Paul, who had vehemently rebelled against Christianity, but then he received a vision of Jesus Christ? On that road to Damascus, it's possible Paul could have been annihilated by the appearance of the Lord. Instead, he was spared by grace. So he repented and returned "grace" for the grace he'd received by taking on a lifelong ministry to testify of Christ. Humbly Paul said, "For I am the least of the apostles, that am not meet to be called an apostle, because I persecuted the church of God. But by the grace of God I am what I am: and his grace which was bestowed upon me was not in vain; but I labored more abundantly than they all: yet not I, but grace of God which was with me" (1 Corinthians 15:9–10).

Black and White

Paul did a complete flip-flop—and I'm not talking about those rubbery sandals people wear. He made an about-face from being a persecutor of Christ to becoming an Apostle of the Lord. He went from darkness to light, from black to white, from sin to salvation.

During my study of the scriptures, I've discovered many verses about darkness being replaced by light—which is part of the "opposition in all things.... even the forbidden fruit in opposition to the tree of life; the one being sweet and the other bitter" (see

2 Nephi 2:11–15). Some folks may like bitter or sour fruit—but bruised and rotten fruit from Satan should be avoided.

For God's children to make correct decisions, the days of our lives require the opposition of good and evil, sin or salvation, right or wrong, sweet or bitter, black or white. However, the scriptures mention nothing about what we might call the "gray areas" of life. This page is printed in black and white—unless you're reading it through rose-colored glasses—because black and white maintain clarity, whether reading books or facing choices in life.

In my befuddled past, I didn't like the idea that everything fell strictly into black or white, with no gray in between. It seemed to put limits on me and what I might do or say. I actually believed it was okay to put myself in a place that seemed to be neither right nor wrong. As a risk-taker, I allowed myself to dabble in what I considered gray territory. I found it exhilarating, because that allowed me to be nearer the black. While on that shadowy edge, I could peer into the things of darkness.

But then I let myself slip. Because I was unable to see clearly in the gray haze, I fell into the blackness of sin. It wasn't until after deep tribulation and repentance that I saw how foolish I'd been. No one can truly be safe while traveling the gray pathways of life, for "strait is the gate, and narrow the way, which leadeth unto life [eternal], and few there be that find it" (Matthew 7:14).

How I shudder now to recall my past misdeeds, especially with these verses:

> I know thy works, that thou art neither cold nor hot: I would thou wert cold or hot.
> So then because thou art lukewarm, and neither cold nor hot, I will spue thee out of my mouth (Revelation 3:16).

We cannot live in a lukewarm fashion. Dabbling in the shadows at the edge of sin is unsafe. Even the twilight of what seems neither good nor bad can be treacherous. Attempting to live in the gray areas of life is risky. Gray is not pure. Gray is not holy. Gray will not bring anyone to "the merits, mercy, and grace of the

Holy Messiah" (2 Nephi 2:8). Only within the Light of Christ can we drink from the fountain of eternal life. "For with thee is the fountain of life: in thy light shall we see light" (Psalms 36:9).

Let the Sun Shine In

During all the decades of my life in Salt Lake City, I've enjoyed walking, jogging, hiking, or biking up City Creek Canyon. I find grandeur in the multifaceted seasons nature offers: icy winter's sparkle, springtime's greening foliage and flowers, summer's lazy days of warmth, and the splendid hues of autumn leaves.

One mid-November day of 45 degrees Fahrenheit, I jogged up City Creek, only to discover that the higher the elevation I reached, the lower dropped the temperature. Wearing a T-shirt and shorts, I began to shiver in the fifth mile, which falls under the shadow of Little Black Mountain.

I kept jogging for one more mile, where I knew the shadow would disperse. When finally I reached the sunlight that beamed brightly into the deep canyon, I stopped and leaned my back against a thick tree trunk. Turning my face upward, I reveled in the sun's warmth. It made me recall a phrase I'd framed on my kitchen wall: "Turn your face to the sun, and the shadows will fall behind you." Then my mind flashed to a tune I'd learned as a child:

> *So let the sun shine in; Face it with a grin.*
> *Smilers never lose, and frowners never win.*
> *So let the sun shine in; Face it with a grin.*
> *Open up your heart and let the sun shine in.*
> (Stuart Hamblen, "Let the Sun Shine In," 1953).

I couldn't help but grin while gazing at the bright blue heavens. How ecstatic to be in the sunlight after jogging through the chilled terrain! That's how I hope to feel at the gates of heaven, after enduring the tribulations of the world. Whether I'm worthy to be ushered through the celestial gates is an even deeper issue.

As I stood that day in the canyon, an inner brilliance lit my soul—the Light of Christ. Unlike the sunlight, I knew the Spirit of the Lord could always be with me, if I would "always remember Him," as the sacramental prayer reminds. Suddenly the phrase from my kitchen wall changed to make it more profound: "Turn your face to the Son (the Son of God) and the shadows will fall behind you."

That childhood tune mentioned above also has more depth in changing sun to Son. When we "Let the Son Shine In," He enlarges our hearts with love and expands our minds with knowledge. The natural effects of such divine influence can spill over to touch others' lives.

As a child, I often gathered armfuls of sunflowers in the fields near our house, then I would take them to my mom. I thought these flowers had received their name because they resemble the sun with round inner disk and yellow petals like sunrays. But that's not the case. They're called sunflowers because each day they face the sun as it rises in the morning, then they follow it through the sky until it sets in the west. When a sunflower no longer keeps its focal point on the sun, it withers and begins to die. The same thing happens to us when we fail to stay focused on Christ.

In the fields where I romped as a child, sunflowers were plentiful, colorful, and easy to pick. Trouble was, I had terrible allergic reactions to sunflowers and would come home sneezing and wheezing. It took considerable scrubbing of my face and hands to rid myself of the dastardly pollen so I could breathe freely again.

Gratefully, I'm not allergic to the Light of Christ. But I wish I were allergic to the "natural man" tendencies that prevent me from gathering additional spiritual blessings. Perhaps I need more frequent scrubbings—called repentance—to rid myself of the weaknesses of the flesh.

Because Latter-day Saints believe that Jesus was born in the northern hemisphere during early April, that means His birth came shortly after the spring solstice. From that day on into summer, the sun rises higher in the sky, increasing the light our hemisphere receives. Indeed, Christ "is the light and life of the world; yea a light that is endless, that can never be darkened; yea and also a life which is endless, that there can be no more death" (Mosiah 16:9). How blessed we are that Jesus illuminates the pathway for us back to our Heavenly Father! As C. S. Lewis stated, "I believe in Christ like I believe in the sun at noonday—not that I can see it, but by it I can see everything else."

When the Father and the Son appeared to Joseph Smith in a pillar of light, they were "above the brightness of the sun," and their "brightness and glory [defied] all description" (Joseph Smith–History 1:16–17). Such radiance should make it easy for anyone to follow Christ, who is the Light of the World.

In English, the dual definition of the word "light" means that Jesus not only provides *light* to guide us, but also He makes our burdens *light* and easy to bear. This doubly lifts our souls and bring us greater joy. It also reminds me of another line from C. S. Lewis: "The reason angels can fly is that they take themselves so lightly."

It is through the grace of God that we live with the potential for a glorious heritage in heaven. Grace is a much broader principle than we realize.

> All those who keep his commandments shall grow up from grace to grace, and become heirs of the heavenly kingdom, and joint heirs with Jesus Christ; possessing the same mind, being transformed into the same image or likeness,... being filled with the fullness of his glory, and become one in him, even as the father, Son and the Holy Spirit are one. [Lectures on Faith 5:2.]

Light in the Wilderness

We're not required to walk in blindness nor darkness, for the Lord's light and grace provide guidance. Our mortal journey is parallel to Lehi's family, when God promised, "I will also be your light in the wilderness; and I will prepare the way before you, if it so be that ye shall keep my commandments; wherefore, inasmuch as ye shall keep my commandments ye shall be led towards the promised land; and ye shall know that it is by me that ye are led"

(1 Nephi 17:13). God also provided unique lighting for the barges in which the Jaredites crossed the dark and troubled seas. I'm intrigued at how the Lord asked that the brother of Jared offer a solution as an answer to his own prayers—a chance to receive grace for grace. Notice in the right-hand column below, how I've modified the verses about the brother of Jared (left column) to apply in our day. Simply put your name in the blank space.

Ether, Chapter 2:	Ether, Chapter 2 (modified for our day):
22 And [the brother of Jared] cried again unto the Lord saying: O Lord, behold I have done even as thou has commanded me; and I have prepared the vessels for my people, and behold there is no light in them. Behold, O Lord, wilt thou suffer that we shall cross this great water in darkness?	22 And _____ cried again unto the Lord saying: O Lord, behold I have done even as thou has commanded me; and I have prepared a home for myself and my family upon this earth, and behold there is no light in our lives. Behold, O Lord, wilt thou suffer that we shall cross this great water in darkness?
23 And the Lord said unto the brother of Jared: What will ye that I should do that ye may have light in your vessels? For behold you cannot have windows, for they will be dashed in pieces; neither shall ye take fire with you, for ye shall not go by the light of fire.	23 And the Lord said unto _____: What will ye that I should do that ye may have light in your lives? For behold you cannot have a window to see heaven, for that knowledge will be veiled; neither shall ye take the God with you in person, for ye cannot go by the light of His glory.

The next verses teach us that when the winds and waves disrupt our lives, God prepares a way to endure them.

Ether, Chapter 2:	Ether, Chapter 2 (modified):
24 For behold ye shall be as a whale in the midst of the sea, for the mountain waves shall dash upon you. Nevertheless, I will bring you up again out of the depths of the sea; for the winds have gone forth out of my mouth, and also the rains and the floods have I sent forth.	24 For behold ye shall be as a child in the midst of a sea of darkness, for the mountain waves of sorrow shall dash upon you. Nevertheless, I will bring you up again out of the depths of darkness; for the winds of adversity have gone forth out of my mouth, and also the trials and the afflictions have I sent forth.
25 And behold, I prepare you against these things; for ye cannot cross this great deep save I prepare you against the waves of the sea, and the winds which have gone forth, and the floods which shall come. Therefore what will ye that I should prepare for you that ye may have light when ye are swallowed up in the depths of the sea?	25 And behold, I prepare you against these things; for ye cannot cross this great darkness on earth save I prepare you against the waves of adversity, and the trials which have gone forth, and the afflictions which shall come. Therefore what will ye that I should prepare for you that ye may have light when ye are swallowed up in the depths of pain and sorrow?

When tossed by waves of adversity and affliction, we must seek counsel from our Father, who has prepared us to withstand these trials.

I marvel that the brother of Jared constantly returned the "grace" of gratitude while he and his people were driven forth in their barges. "And they did sing praises unto the Lord; yea, the brother of Jared did sing praises unto the Lord, and he did thank and praise the Lord all the day long; and when the night came they did not cease to praise the Lord" (Ether 6:9). This is especially stunning because most people would not rejoice while "they were driven forth, three hundred and forty and four days upon the water" (Ether 6:11). That's nearly a whole year! What amazing people, led by the devout brother of Jared, who received grace for grace.

Conclusion

With the spark of divinity instilled in our souls, you and I can become all our Father intends us to be. This is possible when we offer the grace of righteous faith in return for the sanctifying grace of Christ's atonement. Moroni reminds us how to act in order to receive grace: "Yea, come unto Christ, and be perfected in him,... and if ye deny yourselves of all ungodliness, and love God with all your might, mind and strength, then is his grace sufficient for you, that by his grace ye may be perfected in Christ; and if by the grace of God ye are perfect in Christ, ye can in nowise deny the power of God" (Moroni 10:32). Then comes the promise, "if ye by the grace of God are perfect in Christ, and deny not his power, then are ye sanctified in Christ by the grace of God, through the shedding of the blood of Christ, which is in the covenant of the Father unto the remission of your sins, that ye become holy, without spot" (v. 33).

Eternal life is not meant for ogres, demons, centaurs, or other mythical beings. Rather it is offered to the inhabitants of earth who become like Father in Heaven and Jesus Christ. How blessed are those who recognize and arise to their divine heritage!

> Man is made in the image of God himself, so that he can reason, reflect, pray, exercise faith; he can use his energies for the accomplishment of the desires of his heart, and inasmuch as he puts forth his efforts in the proper direction, then he is entitled to an increased portion of the Spirit of the Almighty to inspire him to increased intelligence, to increased prosperity and happiness in the world;...

We must become like God, peradventure to sit upon thrones, to have dominion, power, and eternal increase. God designed this in the beginning.... This is the object of our existence in the world; and we can only attain to these things through obedience to certain principles, through walking in certain channels, through obtaining certain information, certain intelligence from God, without which no man can accomplish his work or fulfill the mission he has come upon the earth to fulfill. [Joseph F. Smith, *Gospel Doctrine*, 62–64.]

For additional insight see:

David A. Bednar, "The Tender Mercies of the Lord," *Ensign*, May. 2005, 99–102.

Grant Von Harrison, *Drawing on the Powers of Heaven*, Publishers Book Sales, Woods Cross, Utah, 1979.

Wist ye not that I must be
about my Father's business?
Luke 2:49

About My Father's Business

Because "the grace of God was upon him," Jesus "waxed strong in Spirit," and was "filled with wisdom" (Luke 2:40). This refers to Christ as a child. It makes me wonder what more I might have accomplished if, as a youngster, I'd been wiser and stronger in Spirit.

Ponder the wisdom Jesus both gave and received at the age of twelve, after attending a Passover feast in Jerusalem. Unbeknownst to His parents, Jesus did not leave to journey home with their family, but instead, He tarried at the temple. After three days of searching, His parents "found him in the temple, sitting in the midst of the doctors, both hearing them, and asking them questions. And all that heard him were astonished at his understanding and answers" (Luke 2:46–47). When His mother, Mary, said they'd sought Jesus with sorrow in their hearts, He replied in a devout manner, "How is it that ye sought me? wist ye not that I must be about my Father's business?" (v. 49).

Twelve is the age when most Latter-day Saint boys are ordained to the Aaronic priesthood. Girls of the same age join the Young Women's program and focus on personal goals of improvement.

Many of our LDS youth faithfully tote their scriptures not only to Sunday meetings, but to seminary classes and family scripture reading. These young men and women are encouraged to "learn wisdom in [their] youth" (Alma 37:35), that they might increase, as Jesus did, "in wisdom and stature, and in favor with God and man" (Luke 2:52).

Wisdom in Maturity

During mid-August of 1999, a tornado swept through the center of Salt Lake City. This is not a normal phenomenon in Utah, as it is in Midwestern states, so it stunned Salt Lakers as well as climatologists. In addition to the turmoil it caused downtown and near the state capitol building, the tornado toppled trees in Memory Grove, before going up the hill where it damaged several homes in the Avenues.

Because I live within a block of Memory Grove, I went to help with cleanup efforts there. I donned leather gloves, thick-soled boots, and protective clothing to toil alongside other volunteers and Red Cross workers. Several of us were assigned to the western slope, where paths and stairs ascend from the grove to the state capitol building. How I marveled at the scene of destruction! Huge trees had splintered into tangles of trunks and limbs. Our task was to wrestle the broken branches free and drag them down to awaiting dump trucks.

Laboring all day long in the hot August air, we consumed gallons of water and other thirst quenchers, as well as high-energy snacks, provided by the Red Cross. The longer we worked, the more the hillside cleared, and we began to notice that a few trees remained intact and undamaged. But they were only small trees. It seemed as if the mature trees had screened the cyclonic wind to shield the younger ones. Taking the brunt of the storm's fury, they willingly sacrificed their majesty so the small trees could continue growing. In like manner, most adults endeavor to protect children and teenagers from harm and foster their development.

Even adults can benefit from the wisdom of more mature individuals. Now in our mid-fifties, my husband and I live in a condominium, where the average age of the residents is more than eighty. Many of our condo neighbors have served as temple presidents, mission presidents, temple workers, and general authorities, including leadership in the general Relief Society. In their exemplary lives throughout the world, they've received wisdom in both temporal and heavenly matters. Though these people might not be steady on their feet, their testimonies are firmly planted on the rock of Jesus Christ. By modeling their examples, I can better teach my own children, grandchildren, and others about life from an eternal perspective.

One day while attending an endowment session at the Salt Lake temple, I sat beside a pair of sweet, white-haired sisters. I fondly remember being taught by them without their realizing it. Before the session began, they briefly chatted. I overheard their conversation, since their whispered voices were loud, due to the hearing loss of old age.

The first sister let out a sigh and said, "It seems like such a long time since we were here."

The second sister smiled, "It feels soooo good to be back."

There was a slight pause, after which the first sister said, "It's been twelve days!"

Twelve days! Stunning! Such intense hunger and thirst these sisters had for righteousness! What loyalty they showed toward the Lord by frequenting His Holy House! Their simple words taught me a tremendous lesson.

Joyful Blessings of the Temple

Each temple is a constant reminder that our earthly lives are not merely for survival but for holy and eternal pursuits. Even in the midst of our everyday temporal routines, the temple can bless us in countless ways.

The endowment which was given by revelation can best be understood by revelation; and to those who seek most vigorously, with pure hearts, will the revelation be greatest. I believe that the busy person on the farm, in the shop, in the office, or in the household, who has his worries and troubles, can solve his problems better and more quickly in the house of the Lord than anywhere else. If he will leave his problems behind, and in the temple work for himself and for his dead, he will confer a mighty blessing upon those who have gone before, and quite as large a blessing will come to him, for at the most unexpected moments, in or out of the temple will come to him, as a revelation, the solution of the problems that vex his life. That is the gift that comes to those who enter the temple properly, because it is a place where revelations may be expected. I bear you my personal testimony that this is true. [John A. Widtsoe, "Temple Worship," *The Utah Genealogical and Historical Magazine*, April 1921, 50–64.]

As someone who enjoys hiking to the top of a mountain, I find special delight when scriptures refer to the temple as "mine holy mountain" (Ezekiel 20:40) or the "mountain of the Lord's house" (Isaiah 2:2–3). I've learned that when I'm busiest—with no apparent spare hours—that's when I especially need to attend the temple. There's no better place to feel the peaceful Spirit of the Lord—it is always a feast of spiritual enlightenment. "And in this mountain shall the Lord of hosts make unto all people a feast of fat [spiritual] things" (Isaiah 25:6). My desire is not to nibble, but to gorge myself on eternal doctrines.

At the temple's abundant feast, I'll ask the Lord to "please pass the peas"; or more correctly, "please pass the P's." Besides the privilege to perform work for the dead, my priorities in the temple are to procure peace, power, prayer, personal revelation, and a permeation of God's love.

Family Togetherness

Whether we're earning our own eternal covenants, endowments, and sealings, or serving those who have died without these ordinances, in the House of God we can both give and receive grace for grace. Not only does the temple convey a nearness to the Lord, but also a closeness to one's family. Parents, grandparents, brothers, sisters, husbands, wives, and other relatives can gather in divine harmony more glorious than any other place on earth. Together, our spirits are elevated to new levels of understanding and compassion for one another. Anyone who has attended a temple wedding or a sealing of children to parents knows it's difficult to restrain tears of eternal joy.

On the day of our wedding, Glenn's blue-gray eyes were radiant as we knelt across the altar from each other. Then the officiator said, "Now Glenn, you will have the rest of your life to look at Bonnie, but during this ceremony you need to look at me."

Besides our wedding day, the most spiritual connection I've felt to Glenn is while doing temple work for ancestors. One evening in the baptismal font, I sensed intense warmth from head to toe— and it wasn't simply the temperature of the water. Glenn stood beside me with his hand raised to the square while he offered the baptismal prayer for one after another of his ancestors. Then He held me securely in his arms while he lowered and raised me in the water. The eternal love we shared increased the connection of our two spirits with the spirits of these ancestors. Not only was my body immersed in water, but also my spirit was immersed in a saturation of divine peace and harmony.

Each Latter-day temple has been dedicated by a prophet or apostle as a house of holiness, "that the Son of Man might have a place to manifest himself to his people" (D&C 109:7). Thus, wherever in the world a temple may be built, there is a calming and tangible spirit felt in the area—by Latter-day Saints as well as nonmembers. Each House of God provides a protective shield that can diminish evil influences and strengthen families.

Make the temple a sacred home away from our eternal home. This temple will be a standing witness that the power of God can stay the powers of evil in our midst. Many parents, in and out of the Church, are concerned about protection against the cascading avalanche of wickedness, which threatens to engulf the world. There is a power associated with the ordinances of heaven, even the power of godliness, which can and will thwart the forces of evil, if we will but be worthy of those sacred covenants made in the temple of the Lord. Our families will be protected, our children will be safeguarded as we live the gospel, visit the temple, and live close to the Lord. [Ezra Taft Benson, *The Teachings of Ezra Taft Benson*, 256.]

What a relief and joy parents feel when their children are married eternally in the temple! After our oldest son and his bride had been sealed, family and friends gathered outside in the garden for photographs. As always, we stood with our group in the temple stairwell behind the happy couple. Before the photographer took one of the shots, he asked the groom to kiss the bride. At the moment they kissed, the bride's veil blew upward with a sudden gust of wind. When later we received the finished photo, we teased our son that his love was so powerful that his kiss made the bride's veil rise. There's no better place to hug and kiss your loved ones than near a temple, which is filled with the radiant power of God's love.

Because one of our God-given gifts is the agency of choice, not every couple gets married in the temple. But as they say in baseball, "It's not over 'til it's over." Parents who keep their temple covenants and raise their children in righteousness have hope of eternal glory for their entire family, as President Lorenzo Snow explained:

God has fulfilled His promises to us, and our prospects are grand and glorious. Yes, in the next life we will have our sons and daughters. If we do not get them all at once, we will have them some time.... You that are mourning about your children straying away will have your sons and your daughters. If you succeed in passing through these trials and afflictions and receive a resurrection, you will, by the power of the Priesthood, work and labor, as the Son of God has, until you get all your sons and daughters in the path of exaltation and glory. This is just as sure as that the sun rose this morning over yonder mountains. Therefore, mourn not because all your sons and daughters do not follow in the path that you have marked out to them, or give heed to your counsels. Inasmuch as we succeed in securing eternal glory, and stand as saviors, and as kings and priests to our God, we will save our posterity. [*Millennial Star*, 22 Jan. 1894, 51–52; see also Boyd K. Packer, "Our Moral Environment," *Ensign*, May 1992, 68.]

Ancient Temple Worship

Throughout past centuries, the temple in Jerusalem was a sacred place of worship and gathering for the Israelites. Prior to that, during their forty-year sojourn with Moses in the wilderness, they had a portable holy edifice called the "tabernacle," used mainly for the rite of sacrificing animals in similitude of Christ's infinite sacrifice. Though we have no record that Adam or Noah built temples, we do know they built sacred altars on which to render offerings to the Lord (see Moses 5:6–7, Genesis 8:20).

It wasn't until the reign of King Solomon when a temple was constructed in Jerusalem for these offerings. That sanctuary was rebuilt several times after contentious wars and destruction. Before and during the time of Christ's ministry, the Roman ruler Herod spent a great deal of time and expense to restore the temple. Though not religious himself, Herod sought to gain favor with the Jewish people.

The initial visit of Jesus to the temple in Jerusalem was as a baby (see Luke 2:22–39). The law of Moses required that the firstborn male of every family must be sanctified unto God (see Exodus 13:2). Throughout His life and ministry, Jesus often visited the temple to preach His new and everlasting gospel.

On one occasion, the Jews gathered in the temple courtyard and asked Him, "How long dost thou make us to doubt? If thou be the Christ, tell us plainly" (John 10:24). Jesus responded by referring to the Father: "I told you, and ye believed not: the works that I do in my Father's name, they bear witness of me" (v. 25).

Everyone sensed Christ's reverence for the Father by how He honored the temple and demanded that others respect it. Twice Jesus reviled against those who brought disgrace to the sacred site with their merchandising. Christ's actions displeased the Jewish leaders, who sought to take Him, but they dared not do it at the temple with so many people watching.

After His gallant prayer in Gethsemane, when Jesus was in solitude, the Jewish leaders and soldiers came quietly to apprehend Him. Jesus said, "I sat daily with you teaching in the temple, and ye laid no hold on me" (Matthew 26:55). Again, during His mock trial, Jesus reminded these unjust leaders, "I ever taught in the synagogue, and in the temple, whither the Jews always resort" (John 18:20).

What a perfect example Jesus set for us to frequent the temple—daily, if it were possible—because that's where to learn many valuable doctrines of salvation.

With Christ's nearness to and fondness for the House of God, it's no wonder at the final moment of His crucifixion that the earth trembled and damaged the temple. "Jesus cried with a loud voice, and gave up the ghost. And the veil of the temple was rent in twain from the top to the bottom" (Mark 15:37–38).

In the Name of Jesus Christ

After Jesus was resurrected and arose into heaven, the apostles continued His legacy of temple worship. As chief among them, Peter knew his ministry was not for his own glory, but was done in the name of Jesus Christ, as in the following scene:

Now Peter and John went up together into the temple at the hour of prayer, being the ninth hour.

And a certain man lame from his mother's womb was carried, whom they laid daily at the gate of the temple which is called Beautiful, to ask alms of them that entered into the temple;

Who seeing Peter and John about to go into the temple asked an alms.

And Peter, fastening his eyes upon him with John, said, Look on us.

And he gave heed unto them, expecting to receive something of them.

Then Peter said, Silver and gold have I none; but such as I have give I thee: In the name of Jesus Christ of Nazareth rise up and walk.

And he took him by the right hand, and lifted him up; and immediately his feet and ankle bones received strength.

And he leaping up stood, and walked, and entered with them into the temple, walking and leaping, and praising God.

And all the people saw him walking and praising God (Acts 3:1–9).

What simple, yet profound words Peter spoke: "Silver and gold have I none, but such as I have, give I thee." Though not endowed with temporal wealth, Peter was empowered by the Spirit of the Lord. With confidence, he looked upon the lame man and commanded, "In the name of Jesus Christ of Nazareth rise up and walk."

What a treasured example for us to follow! Though we may be unable to offer earthly treasures, we can extend a helping hand to those in need. We can share the riches of the gospel with them, and lift them toward spiritual healing through the power of the Atonement. Then, like the lame man Peter healed, they can leap forward in life by praising and worshiping God in the holy temple.

Latter-day Temples

Unlike Biblical times, we no longer sacrifice burnt offerings in today's temples. Now we partake of ordinances, covenants, endowments, sealings, and other sacred procedures. Temples have often required sacrifices to construct them—in Biblical times as well as in the latter days. The Saints in Kirtland and Nauvoo willingly gave their time, health, and wealth in order to receive temple blessings.

The dedication Joseph offered for the Kirtland temple was the start of many prayers to sanctify latter-day temples for the work of God. "And that all people who shall enter upon the threshold of the Lord's house may feel thy power.... And we ask thee, Holy Father, that thy servants may go forth from this house armed with thy power, and that thy name may be upon them, and thy glory be round about them, and thine angels have charge over them" (D&C 109:13, 22).

Armed with God's power! Glory around us! Christ's name upon us! Angels have charge over us! What hallowed blessings can be ours if we faithfully attend the temple. After that memorable dedication, Jesus Christ came in person to accept the Kirtland temple: "We saw the Lord standing upon the breastwork of the pulpit, before us;... His eyes were as a flame of fire; the hair of his head was white like the pure snow; his countenance shone above the brightness of the sun" (D&C 110:2–3).

Attending the temple is not about keeping score to see if you can go more often than your neighbor. Rather, our success is measured in spiritual advancement as we receive instruction, comfort, worship, revelation, edification, and sublime blessings. If, like the lame man whom Peter healed at the temple, we feel crippled by trials or burdened with grief, temple worship can help heal us. Even those who cannot enter the temple, because of illness or unworthiness, can prayerfully face the temple and plead for deliverance. This is clear in President Wilford Woodruff's dedication of the Salt Lake Temple:

Heavenly Father, when Thy people shall not have the opportunity of entering this holy house... and they are oppressed and in trouble, surrounded by difficulties or assailed by temptation and shall turn their faces towards this Thy holy house and ask Thee for deliverance, for help, for Thy power to be extended in their behalf, we beseech Thee, to look down from Thy holy habitation in mercy and tender compassion upon them, and listen to their cries. Or when the children of Thy people, in years to come,... shall cry unto Thee from the depths of their affliction and sorrow to extend relief and deliverance to them, we humbly entreat Thee to turn Thine ear in mercy to them; hearken to their cries, and grant unto them the blessings for which they ask. [N. B. Lundwall, *Temples of the Most High*, 128.]

As we strive to survive the perils prophesied in the last days, we should seek the protection and security available when we "stand in holy places" (D&C 45:32), of which the temples are paramount.

> The temple ceremonies are designed by a wise Heavenly Father who has revealed them to us in these last days as a guide and protection throughout our lives, that you and I might not fail of an exaltation in the celestial kingdom where God and Christ dwell.
>
> We talk about security in this day, and yet we fail to understand that here in this temple block we have standing the holy temple wherein we may find the symbols by which power might be generated that will save this nation from destruction. [Harold B. Lee, *Teachings of Harold B. Lee*, 342.]

Power in the temple to save this nation from destruction. That's a valuable promise. This clearly demonstrates that not only are spiritual blessing poured out following temple worship, but also temporal blessings await us.

Admission to the temple is free—except for the price we pay to repent and become worthy to enter. That means we can't bribe a priesthood leader into giving us a temple recommend—no more than we can bribe God into giving us blessings. Our Father in Heaven does not want to exclude anyone from entering His Holy House, but He knows we cannot feel the Spirit there unless we are pure before Him. The questions we're required to answer during interviews with our leaders are meant to increase our level of spirituality before we visit the temple.

Have you ever had someone ask to borrow your temple recommend? I did. She was a good friend, but she hadn't been an active member for many years. Her question was meant to be a joke. But it didn't make me laugh. Tenets of the Church are not to be trifled with nor laughed at. My temple recommend is the most valuable item in my wallet. I plan to keep it safe until I die. Perhaps even then, it can be tucked into a corner of my casket.

Temple Service

Though President Howard W. Hunter served only nine short months as our prophet, he did a manifold job in turning our hearts toward the importance of temple service. He counseled members of the Church that temple worship not only provides more understanding of the purpose of everyday life, but it also prepares us for the millennial reign of Christ:

> I invite the Latter-day Saints to look to the temple of the Lord as the great symbol of your membership....
>
> As we attend the temple, we learn more richly and deeply the purpose of life and the significance of the atoning sacrifice of the Lord Jesus Christ. Let us make the temple, with temple worship and temple covenants and temple marriage, our ultimate earthly goal and the supreme mortal experience.
>
> May you let the meaning and beauty and peace of the temple come into your everyday life more directly in order that the millennial day may come. [Howard W. Hunter, "Exceeding Great and Precious Promises," *Ensign*, Nov. 1994, 8–9.]

Each house of God has a direct impact on the Savior's Second Coming. I wonder if that's why President Gordon B. Hinckley has been constructing additional temples throughout the world at a phenomenal rate. Now, more Latter-day Saints can receive eternal ordinances nearer to home.

During November of 2005, I went with my husband to visit our son's family in Hong Kong. While there, we attended an endowment session at the temple. Because Hong Kong is a city with people of many nationalities, we were not surprised to be the only Caucasians in the room. It wasn't until the session ended that we discovered we'd been with a group from Sri Lanka who came to spend an entire week at the temple. They'd traveled more than 2,500 miles from their home. Most had never flown in an airplane.

It took over a year for these thirteen men, women, and a few children to prepare for the trip—starting with temple preparation classes, paying a full tithing, committing to more fully keep the commandments, and saving rupees to cover their expenses. Then each received a temple recommend from the Singapore Mission President. However, their visiting Hong Kong was delayed while awaiting their passports from the Sri Lankan government and approval for the trip by the Area Presidency.

When finally they arrived in Hong Kong, many were awed by the skyscrapers all lit up at night for the holiday season. Some also had new experiences riding an escalator and a double-decker bus. But nothing compared to the glorious emotions they felt upon entering the temple the next morning. Their dreams were fulfilled as, day after day, they completed initiatory ordinances, endowments, and sealings for themselves and many ancestors. Besides doing work for their families, they performed baptisms and other temple ordinances as proxy for hundreds of Chinese people who died without knowledge of the truth.

The Sri Lankan's commitment and joy were evident as they gathered in the celestial room after the endowment session. Their sacrifices to attend the temple brought eternal blessings upon each individual, as well as their ancestors, posterity, and the Chinese.

Conclusion

I admire the tenacity of those Saints from Sri Lanka, particularly since I'm privileged to live within a few blocks of the Salt Lake Temple. I rarely make any sacrifices to attend session, except to face an occasional blizzard walking there in the winter. Whether close to home or traveling to other locations, I am blessed and edified with each temple experience.

Receiving eternal ordinances is our only hope to obtain eternal exaltation. We cannot buy our way into the celestial kingdom. We couldn't possibly afford it. Only the Savior could pay the price. He gave His very life to save us. Perhaps we ought to give Him something in return. Suggested gifts are honestly, loyalty, faith, love, gratitude, and service. Giving up our pride might also be requisite to entering into His rest.

At the age of twelve, Jesus declared, "I must be about my father's business" (Luke 2:49). Those of us who didn't begin to serve God at such a tender age may need to redouble our efforts. Otherwise, we may be begging for entrance into the celestial kingdom, "Please, oh, pretty please, with sugar and cream on it!"

Gratefully, the Lord is merciful and compassionate. While living on earth, Jesus rendered everything within His power for our sake—including His ignominious death. From before the foundation of this world, He vowed to carry forth the plan to redeem all our Father's children. And forevermore throughout eternity, our Redeemer will work unceasingly for the salvation of every son and daughter of God.

How glorious that we are given opportunities to help others attain salvation and exaltation! May we prayerfully, humbly, and enthusiastically assist in this sublime endeavor. Jesus has already earned His eternal reward. May we follow His example and do the same.

For additional insight see:

Robert D. Hales, "The Message: What Think Ye of Christ?", *New Era*, April 1987, 4–7.

Boyd K. Packer, *That All May Be Edified*, Salt Lake City, Bookcraft, 1982, 234–235.

Boyd K. Packer, *The Holy Temple*, Salt Lake City, Bookcraft, 1980.

Temples of The Church of Jesus Christ of Latter-day Saints, Salt Lake City, Intellectual Reserve, 1999

Harold B. Lee, *Stand Ye in Holy Places*, Salt Lake City, Deseret Book, 1974.

Ensign, February, 2007, 12–23.

And the apostles said unto the Lord,
Increase our faith.
Luke 17:5

Increase  Our Faith

In the Fourth Article of Faith we learn that the first principle of the gospel is: "faith in the Lord Jesus Christ" ("The Articles of Faith," *Pearl of Great Price*, 61). Faith is not something you can get from your favorite mail-order catalogue: $19.95 plus shipping and handling. Faith in Christ can only be achieved with determination and perseverance. "Faith is things which are hoped for and not seen; wherefore, dispute not because ye see not, for ye receive no witness until after the trial of your faith" (Ether 12:60). Some people say you can have "too much of a good thing." But where faith is concerned, that's not the case.

When the Twelve Apostles "said unto the Lord, Increase our faith" (Luke 17:5), He replied, "If ye had faith as a grain of mustard seed, ye might say unto this sycamine tree, Be thou plucked up by the root, and be thou planted in the sea, and it should obey you" (v. 6). His efforts to teach God's children how to practice and perform faith-based miracles is as pertinent today as it was in that time.

Faith and fear cannot coexist. Faith in Jesus Christ is the antithesis of fear. Where faith is lacking, fear can cause cracks in our pipeline to heaven. Yet Jesus admonished, "Look unto me in every thought, doubt not, fear not" (D&C 6:36). When fear destabilizes and debilitates our faith, we need to call in a plumber to patch the holes in our spiritual pipeline. The Holy Ghost, who bears witness of the Father and Son, is the best fix-it man I know. Through His whispered voice, we remember Christ's words of comfort, "Be of good cheer, and do not fear, for I the Lord am with you, and will stand by you" (D&C 68:6).

Most Latter-day Saints have the faith necessary to attend church, serve in callings, and look with hope toward eternal life. Some individuals receive the spiritual gift of "exceedingly great faith" (Moroni 10:11). After King Benjamin delivered his profound address, the multitude who heard his words fell to their knees to plead that God would purify their hearts through the Savior's redemption. Then "after they had spoken these words the Spirit of the Lord came upon them... because of the *exceeding faith* which they had in Jesus Christ" (Mosiah 4:2–3, italics added).

Even if your faith seems thin and fragile like pastry dough, it is always sweet to the taste; however, faith can get stale and crusty without constant attention. It's that principle of "Blessed are all they who do hunger and thirst after righteousness, for they shall be filled with the Holy Ghost" (3 Nephi 12:6). The Holy Ghost is the bearer of gifts of the spirit, and faith is a prime gift for which we should hunger and thirst.

I am blessed to live in a manner that I rarely go hungry— unless I'm fasting or dieting. It's interesting that my fasting has always been more productive than my dieting.

Have you ever been plagued by unquenchable thirst? Lost in a desert with nothing but mirages? I recall a day of extreme thirst while hiking in the mountains north of Durango, Colorado. The morning was cool when I began the trek, but as the sun rose higher in the sky, I began to perspire. Soon my meager water supply was gone. By the time I reached a summit between two peaks, my throat was parched, and my entire body began to plead for water. I chewed a few candies in hopes they would replenish me, but that only increased my thirst. I ached, craved, yearned, anguished and languished for a drink. I knew that even if I turned around to go back down the trail, my body would still need water.

Then I saw it! A tiny spring bubbled from the base of a rock. Though just a trickle, it was enough that I could cup my hands and fill them. I gulped the cool water like a camel at an oasis. How refreshing! What a miracle! At least that's how I saw it at the time. I sent a silent prayer heavenward, then filled my water bottle. Though I never reached a critical, life-threatening state, those moments of craving taught me what it means to hunger and thirst after righteousness.

Whether the adversity we face is lack of water or lack of spirituality, we can better withstand our trials when we build our faith "upon the rock of our Redeemer, who is Christ, the Son of God" (Helaman 5:12). Jesus taught a parable about the wise man who built his house upon a rock. Even though the winds and rains beat upon the house, "it fell not: for it was founded upon a rock" (Matthew 7:25).

Those who don't have a foundation of faith might have "a great fall," as did Humpty Dumpty and the foolish man in the parable. Rather than building on the rock of Christ, the foolish man placed his house in the shifting sands of the world. Then came the rain and floods, "and beat upon that house; and it fell: and great was the fall of it" (v. 27).

We all make choices in life—some foolish and some wise. In every instance, we can either heed and act upon the doctrines of Christ, or we can choose to hearken to other voices. No source but God offers to "multiply a multiplicity of blessings" to the righteous (D&C 97:28). Yet, many deny their need for God, and they impatiently say, "Forget the blessings. I need cash. I need it now."

I was stunned by a brief news poll taken at the end of December, 2006: "In a British survey, 2,500 children under age ten were asked, 'What do you think is the very best thing in the world?'

The number one answer was 'Money and getting rich,' followed by 'Being famous.' 'God' was number ten." [*The Real Truth* magazine; Jan. 2007, 24.]

It's frightening to think that these children, under age ten, have already had their values warped by prideful desires to be rich and famous. With Satan's influence, our world has become increasingly more aggressive, haughty, prideful, and boisterous. The cacophony makes it difficult to hear the still small voice calling us to faith, righteousness, and peace. "But learn that he who doeth the words of righteousness shall receive his reward, even peace in this world and eternal life in the world to come" (D&C 59:23).

What Faith Is

Paul's epistle to the Hebrews states, "Now faith is the substance of things hoped for, the evidence of things not seen" (Hebrews 11:1). A friend of mine, who no longer attends church, once argued that faith cannot be *substance* because it is intangible. Nor can it be *evidence* since it's not visible and presentable as facts. I beg to differ. Paul's epistle states that "through faith we understand that the worlds were framed by the word of God, so that things which are seen were not made of things which do appear" (v. 3). He then shares how several individuals produced grand results from faith: Abel, Enoch, Noah, Abraham and his wife Sarah, Isaac, Jacob, Joseph, Moses, "of David also, and Samuel, and of the prophets" (v. 32). Then Paul lists actions resulting from these people's faith: "Who through faith subdued kingdoms, wrought righteousness, obtained promises, stopped the mouths of lions, quenched the violence of fire, escaped the edge of the sword, out of weakness were made strong, waxed valiant in fight.... Women received their dead raised to life again" (vv. 33–35).

All these acts, recorded in the Bible, were performed by faith. Surely, that is *evidence* of the *substance* of faith.

I believe faith is energy. According to Albert Einstein, $E=MC^2$, which means energy equals mass [matter] multiplied by velocity squared (actually the square of the speed of light). Like the unseen wind, faith is felt in various strengths from tiny bursts of hope to magnanimous miracles. Just as a mind's idea can bring forth an invention which was previously unknown, faith is the power to perform tasks and miracles which may seem beyond human limitations. Faith can produce spiritual manifestations such as visions, healings, the gift on tongues, and other miracles. It requires actions, words of trust, and well-directed thoughts to see results of our faith.

We learn from experience that faith won't give us an "A" on an exam for which we haven't diligently studied. Nor will faith help a person succeed on the TV show "American Idol," especially if he or she has no talent. Faith in Jesus Christ is usually focused on endeavors with eternal significance.

Moroni wrote, "By faith all things are fulfilled... For if there be no faith among the children of men God can do no miracle among them" (Ether 12:3, 12). Later, he recounts his father Mormon's words about faith: "And Christ hath said: If ye will have faith in me ye shall have power to do whatsoever thing is expedient in me.... For it is by faith that miracles are wrought;... wherefore, if these things have ceased wo be unto the children of men, for it is because of unbelief" (Moroni 7:33, 35).

So have miracles ceased because we have no faith? Not on your life! Though we don't see Elijah calling fire from heaven to consume an altar's sacrifice, nor Moses parting the Red Sea, today's Saints witness miracles pertinent to our day and age: restoration of health, expansion of family history research, building of temples, and spreading the gospel throughout the world.

Faith and Works

Faith is not a stagnant principle. It involves action and good works. High priests are ordained "on account of their *exceeding faith and good works*" (Alma 13:3, italics added). Whether or not they sleep in Church is not taken into account.

Many of us are familiar with how James explained that "as the body without the spirit is dead, so faith without works is dead also" (see James 2:14–26). Though we may claim to have unmatched faith in Jesus Christ and pray unceasingly to our Father, if we fail to *do* the will of God, we'll fail to enter heaven. "Not every one that saith unto me, Lord, Lord, shall enter into the kingdom of heaven;

but he that *doeth the will of my Father* which is in heaven" (Matthew 7:21, italics added).

Tapping into divine power is made possible through our faith—the more the better. Whether we exercise faith as a vast community or merely a single individual, our Father in Heaven can then empower us with courage to do His will. It's not that we'll become robots enabled by God's remote control. But rather, through our faith we are granted divine spiritual gifts to build His kingdom. One of my favorite thoughts states, "It is not the greatness of my faith that moves mountains, but my faith in the greatness of God."

Because Nephi, the son of Helaman, "with unwearyingness declared the word," God made him "mighty in word, and in deed, in faith, and in works" (Helaman 10:4–5). Our Father knew Nephi would not ask for anything contrary to His will, therefore, he was granted "power, that whatsoever ye shall seal on earth shall be sealed in heaven; and whatsoever ye shall loose on earth shall be loosed in heaven; and thus shall ye have power among this people" (v. 7).

Because the people refused to repent of their wickedness, Nephi sealed the heavens to withhold rain through "the power of God [that] was with him" (v 16). Many perished in the ensuing famine, until Nephi finally petitioned the Lord to again send rain (see Helaman 10 and 11).

Imagine having the power to say, "rain, rain, go away," and then see it fulfilled! How popular I might have been to perform such a feat, especially in the midst of a crucial high school football game. Perhaps I could also have caused a small tornado to sweep the opposing team off their feet, so we could score record-breaking touchdowns. But alas, miracles aren't meant to increase popularity, but rather to benefit the kingdom of God.

One Nephite prophet wrote, "our faith becometh unshaken, insomuch that we truly can command in the name of Jesus and the very trees obey us, or the mountains, or the waves of the sea" (Jacob 4:6). These people were mere humans, but infused with divine power because of their unshakable faith in God. Each righteous individual has the potential to command miraculous changes on earth. But instead, many of us allow the cares of the world to command us.

Faith is vital in nourishing the word of God so it might grow from a seed into a tree with abundant fruit. As explained in Alma 32, you can "compare the word [of God] unto a seed... planted in your heart" (v. 28). Through faith, your seed will sprout and grow, expanding your soul until it becomes pure knowledge. Then "if ye will nourish the word [of God], yea, nourish the tree as it beginneth to grow, *by your faith with great diligence*," it will spring "up into everlasting life" (v. 41).

After the resurrection, a lesson in faith was offered to Thomas, who was absent when Jesus appeared to the other Apostles. After inviting Thomas to touch His wounded body as proof that He was real, the Lord admonished, "be not faithless, but believing.... Jesus saith unto him, Thomas, because thou hast seen me, thou hast believed: blessed are they that have not seen, and yet have believed" (John 20:27, 29). Perhaps all of God's children need frequent reminders to "be not faithless, but believing."

Help Thou Mine Unbelief

Consider the humble father who brought his stricken son to Jesus for healing. "Jesus saith unto him, If thou canst believe, all things are possible to him that believeth." Then "straightway the father of the child cried out, and said with tears, Lord, I believe; help thou mine unbelief" (Mark 9:23–24). Sometimes it takes tears and pleading to strengthen our belief in the Lord. Directly after Jesus healed this stricken boy, the disciples came privately to ask Jesus, "Why could not we cast him out?" His response was memorable. "This kind can come forth by nothing, but by prayer and fasting" (vv. 28–29). Because "the spirit indeed is willing, but the flesh is weak" (Matthew 26:41), our efforts to heal others—in physical, emotional, or spiritual ways—might need the boost that fasting and prayer bring.

The sons of Mosiah showed us it's often necessary to study, pray, and fast to increase faith in the power of God. "They searched the scriptures diligently, that they might know the word of God. But this was not all; they had given themselves to much prayer and fasting; therefore they had the spirit of prophecy, and the spirit of revelation, and… they taught with power and authority of God" (Alma 17:2–3).

In these days of instant therapy, it's easy to view Dr. Phil on the television or hear Dr. Laura on the radio. Both of these therapists have helped countless numbers of people; yet they could be even more effective healers if their therapy also focused on steadfast faith in Christ.

Remember the faith of the woman with the "issue of blood"? For twelve years, she had been plagued with ill health. Though she frequently visited physicians, she never found a cure. Then, hearing about Jesus Christ, this woman earnestly sought Him, for she thought, "If I may touch but his clothes, I shall be whole" (Mark 5:28). What remarkable faith! Unable to get His attention in the crowded streets of Jerusalem, this woman came up behind Him and touched His garment. "And straightway the fountain of her blood was dried up" (v. 29).

When Jesus asked who had touched him, the disciples scoffed because of the crushing throng of people. Yet with remarkable sensitivity to the "one" individual who needed Him, Jesus turned and said, "Daughter, thy faith hath made thee whole; go in peace and be whole of thy plague" (v. 34).

On another occasion, beside the pool of Bethesda, "lay a multitude of impotent folk, of blind, halt, withered, waiting for the moving of the water." They believed when the water was stirred by an angel, the first person who entered the pool would be restored to health (see John 5:3–4). What faith to wait day after day, and often year after year, for a turn to be healed!

One man, burdened with an infirmity thirty-eight years, had no one to help him get into the pool for healing. But Jesus came and "saith unto him, Wilt thou be made whole?" (John 5:6) What a question to hear after thirty-eight years of afflictions! "Wilt thou be made whole?" Perhaps in a similar way, Jesus offers to make each of us whole, whether we suffer from feebleness of the body or frailties of the spirit. Though we often focus on Christ's miracles of curing physical ailments, His deeper intent is to make us spiritually whole, or holy. Through faith, we can arise and feel the Lord's power of healing when He says, as He did to the man beside the pool, "Rise, take up thy bed [of affliction], and walk" (v. 8).

Faith Is an Anchor

The Prophet Moroni compared faith to an anchor: "Wherefore, whoso believeth in God might with surety hope for a better world, yea, even a place at the right hand of God, which hope cometh of faith, maketh an anchor to the souls of men, which would make them sure and steadfast, always abounding in good works, being led to glorify God" (Ether 12:4). Notice again that faith is tied to good works.

Made of heavy metal, an anchor is attached to the ship by a thick cable or chain, just as we should be linked to Christ by our faith. Used more often in a harbor than in the open sea, an anchor's job is to keep a ship from drifting away from safety, therefore, the people and cargo remain "sure and steadfast."

The stem of the anchor supports a curved cross piece with pointed ends that wedge into a foundation beneath the ship. Typically an anchor is viewed with the curved portion pointed downward, because that's how it is raised and lowered from the ship. But if you turn that anchor upside down and straighten the curved piece, it closely resembles a cross. That reminds us that Jesus will sustain us against any wild tides or undercurrents that might endeavor to unsteady our moorings.

Those who put their faith in Christ and trust Him to change their souls can receive peace in their hearts, even if pandemonium rages in the world. Faith provides impetus to purify our lives, or in other words, to assist us with "a mighty change in us, or in our hearts, that we have no more disposition to do evil, but to do good continually" (Mosiah 5:2). President Ezra Taft Benson offered the following insight of how Christ can change human nature:

When you choose to follow Christ,
You choose to be changed....
The Lord works from the inside out.
The world works from the outside in.
The world would take people out of the slums.
Christ takes the slums out of people,
And then they take themselves out of the slums.
The world would mold men by changing their environment.
Christ changes men, who then change their environment.
The world would shape human behavior.
But Christ can change human nature....
Christ changes men.
And changed men can change the world.
[Ezra Taft Benson, "Born of God," *Ensign*, Nov. 1985, 5–7,
paragraphing altered.]

Prayers of Faith

While in Jerusalem, our group went to the palace of Caiaphas, where Jesus was arraigned in a contemptuous fashion. The tour would require descending ladders and staircases to view the stony dungeon where Jesus was cruelly incarcerated. Because there were already too many people on the narrow staircases in the building, our group had to sit in a covered courtyard to await our turn.

Soon we heard voices arising from the corridors below us, and then a series of people began to ascend the ladder to the courtyard. From their conversations we discerned they were American Christians—yet they were quite unique for a group of travelers. Most of them were blind. Some had patches over their eyes, others wore glasses with thick lenses, and several held white canes to feel their way forward. A few were assisted by sighted persons at their sides. How I marveled at their faith! They'd come all the way from America to Jerusalem without the ability to see the sacred sites.

One man in my group leaned over and whispered to me, "Wouldn't it be great if we had enough faith that we could lay our hands on their heads and heal their blindness?"

"Yes," I said, marveling at his idea. I wondered how much faith it would take to heal them one by one. The thought barely had time to incubate in my mind before the blind people were gone out the door to their buses. Later, I discovered several scriptures that reveal how faith and prayer are eternally entwined:

> And the Spirit shall be given unto you by the prayer of faith (D&C 42:14).
> It should be granted unto them according to their faith in their prayers (D&C 10:47).
> Look unto God with firmness of mind, and *pray unto him with exceeding faith*, and he will console you in your afflictions (Jacob 3:1, italics added).

Offering a sincere prayer is not something we can pretend to do, unless we want to get pretend blessings in return. Prayer is the conduit to our Father in Heaven, who should be reverenced and honored in all we say.

After witnessing Christ's prayers, His disciples were eager to learn more about prayer. "And it came to pass, that, as he was praying in a certain place, when he ceased, one of his disciples said unto him, Lord, teach us to pray," (Luke 11:1). He then instructed His disciples through what is called the Lord's Prayer. At both the beginning and end of His prayer, Jesus reverenced His Father: "Hallowed be thy name.... For thine is the kingdom, and the power, and the glory, forever. Amen" (see Matthew 6:9–13). Thus Jesus gave us the pattern: Our prayers are meant to ascend to our Father in Heaven, but we offer them in the name of Jesus Christ, who "is even at the right hand of God, who also maketh intercession for us" (Romans 8:34).

During Christ's visit to the Promised Land, He suggested we follow His example in prayer. "Behold, I am the light; I have set an example for you.... Behold ye see that I have prayed unto the Father, and ye all have witnessed" (3 Nephi 18:16, 24). Try to imagine being in the Promised Land when the multitude heard Jesus offer words so sacred they could not be recorded.

Behold he prayed unto the Father, and the things which he prayed cannot be written, and the multitude did bear record who heard him.

And after this manner do they bear record: The eye hath never seen, neither hath the ear heard, before, so great and marvelous things as we saw and heard Jesus speak unto the Father;

And no tongue can speak, neither can there be written by any man, neither can the hearts of men conceive so great and marvelous things as we both saw and heard Jesus speak; and no one can conceive of the joy which filled our souls at the time we heard him pray for us unto the Father (3 Nephi 17:15–17).

Praying Aloud

Prayers at church meetings or within our families are vocalized so everyone can pronounce an "Amen" at the end. Prayers unites us in love and compassion for one another, and more importantly, they unify us with our Heavenly Father. Though prayers should be offered with reverence, I'm certain our Father keeps a sense of humor as He hears our human ramblings. Once, a woman praying at the start of our choir practice forgot the organist's name, so in the midst of her prayer, she said, "And bless what's-his-bucket at the organ." I could barely stifle my laughter.

Personal prayers are best in a private, secluded place. My husband and I have family prayer each evening, but we go to separate locations for our personal prayers. If I wait until the moment before falling into bed, fatigue often clouds my mind, so I often pray earlier than bedtime. Praying aloud is also more fulfilling—more of a conversation with the Father, rather than just "saying prayers."

Our Father does not have an answering machine for us to leave a quick message. He will personally take each call. He won't screen anyone out with caller I.D. Nor does He refuse phone solicitations. In fact, God welcomes all solicitations for sustenance and appeals for guidance. After prayer, during the silence of our heart, is when God speaks comfort and wisdom to our souls. It is said that "prayer is when we communicate with our Father, and meditation is when He communicates with us."

Most of us have heard children utter unusual prayers, such as, "Please bless that I won't have to eat my vegetables, because I hate broccoli," or "Bless that the tooth fairy will leave me a dollar instead of a quarter." Even adults sometimes struggle with proper prayer language, for we are supposed to use *Thee, Thou,* or *Thy* to refer to God, instead of *You* or *Your.* Proper prayer takes practice, persistence, and perseverance.

Some people offer prayers that are repetitive, using the same words time after time. That's like being stuck in neutral—rarely going anywhere in our prayers. I suppose that's better than being stuck in reverse: moving downhill from heartfelt communing with our Father to using rushed and trite phrases.

That reminds me of our old Chevy Nova, which was the first car Glenn and I bought as a married couple. As the car aged, it became stubborn and persnickety—always when I was in a hurry to get some place. One day while serving as a counselor in our ward Primary presidency, I rushed my four small children into the car for Tuesday afternoon Primary. After backing the Nova out of the garage and driveway, I grabbed the stick shift and tried to move the standard transmission into forward drive. But it would not budge out of reverse. I pushed and pounded on the gear shift, and I even made an attempt to shove it with my foot. Nothing worked. I knew it was too late to get out the stroller or wagon and walk with my four children to the church. So I did the only feasible thing with a car stuck in reverse: I drove backwards the up the hill and through the neighborhood to get to Primary. When the meeting ended, I also had to drive in reverse on the way home. Needless to say, the Nova went to get transmission service the very next day. So if our prayers get stuck in reverse or even in neutral, it may be time to make repairs. Prayer repair.

When possible, it's best to kneel when we pray, though that gets increasingly difficult as we age. After knee surgery, following a harsh tumble on the ski slopes, I couldn't kneel for several months. But that makes it all the more meaningful to me now. Though I'm on the ground, it seems as if I'm standing tall, because the Spirit lifts my thoughts heavenward. During prayer my eyes are closed, yet I can see eternal goals with more clarity. Blinding temptations disappear, and the power of God helps me view my life through spiritual eyes. When I seek a secluded place for prayer, the riotous noise of the world fades away, then I can better attune to the Spirit's whispered voice. Being on my knees also makes it is easier to lay down my burdens and share them with the Lord, rather than holding onto them. How blessed we are to humbly bow before our Father to seek His wisdom and mercy!

Prayer in Our Hearts

When we cannot drop to our knees and pray vocally, we're admonished to keep a prayer in our hearts. "Yea, and when you do not cry [aloud] unto the Lord, let your hearts be full, drawn out in prayer unto him continually for your welfare, and also for the welfare of those who are around you" (Alma 34:27). Ofttimes, we're more inclined to pray when scathed by adversity. Yet an essential part of prayer is thanking our Father in Heaven for our blessings, "name them one by one. Count your many blessings; See what God hath done." ["Count Your Blessings," *Hymns*, 241.]

If prayer is only a spasmodic cry at the time of crisis, then it is utterly selfish, and we come to think of God as a repairman or a service agency to help us only in our emergencies. We should remember the Most High day and night—always—not only at times when all other assistance has failed and we desperately need help. If there is any element in human life on which we have a record of miraculous success and inestimable worth to the human soul, it is prayerful, reverential, devout communication with our Heavenly Father....

Perhaps what this world needs is to "look up" as the Psalmist said (Psalm 5:1–33)—to look up in our joys as well as our afflictions, in our abundance as well as in our needs. We must continually look up and acknowledge God as the giver of every good thing and the source of our salvation. [Howard W. Hunter, "Hallowed Be Thy Name," *Ensign*, Nov. 1977, 52.]

Our Father already knows our needs before we petition Him, for He can foresee the various obstacles and roadblocks we may encounter. If we find ourselves unsure of what to pray for, just listen to the Spirit's promptings:

> Likewise the Spirit also helpeth our infirmities: for we know not what we should pray for ought; but the Spirit itself maketh intercession for us with groanings which cannot be uttered
> And he that searcheth the hearts... maketh intercessions for the saints according to the will of God (Romans 8:26–27).

Prayers that are quick and casual may not produce the answers and blessings we desire. Just as faith and works go hand in hand, so do prayer and works. We must "work out [our] own salvation" (Mormon 9:27) by exerting faith in Christ and calling upon our Father for guidance—whether praying alone, with family, or in other settings.

Conclusion

How much our spirituality might increase if, like the ancient apostles, we petition the Lord to "increase our faith," and "teach us to pray." It is in the midst of our deepest prayers that our faith in God expands.

> Whatsoever thing ye shall ask the Father in my name, which is good, in faith believing that ye shall receive, behold, it shall be done unto you.... If ye will have faith in me ye shall have power to do whatsoever thing is expedient in me (Moroni 7:26, 33).

More than anyone else, Jesus knows what it means to kneel in fervent prayer. I have seen the gnarled olive trees in Gethsemane, where Christ's soul was gnarled and broken as He submitted to the Father by saying "thy will be done." Perhaps these are the most awe-inspiring words ever spoken on earth.

It is through faith in Christ and prayer to our Father that They shares our lives—the joys and the sorrows, the failures and triumphs. Most of us are still learning to say, "Thy will be done." Yet even if our faith seems weak and our prayers are stuck in neutral, remember the comforting words Jesus spoke to Peter, "I have prayed for thee that thy faith fail not" (Luke 22:32). No doubt He earnestly prays for each one of us.

For addition insight see:
Howard W. Hunter, "Hallowed Be Thy Name," Ensign, Nov. 1977, 52-54.
Neal A. Maxwell, *Lord, Increase Our Faith*, Bookcraft, Salt Lake City.

And ye shall know the truth,
and the truth shall make you free.
John 8:42

The Truth Shall Make You Free

In the title of this chapter, I almost omitted "The," but it didn't sound complete—rather like a popsicle without a stick. It's not general truth, such as mathematical equations and scientific facts, that make the children of God free, but "The Truth" of the gospel of Jesus Christ. When we "know *the truth,… the truth* shall make [us] free" (John 8:42, italics added). How exactly does the truth make us free? One clue is revealed in this verse: "Jesus saith unto him, I am the way, the truth, and the life: no man cometh unto the Father, but by me" (John 14:6). Jesus Christ is *the truth*. It is through our Savior's teachings and our reliance on His Atonement that we become free—free from sin, sorrow, grief, and pain—but only to the degree that we repent and plead for His healing love.

Latter-day doctrine has revealed that all truth, whether religious or secular, is governed through our omniscient Father in Heaven. Though He comprehends all things, it's not necessary for us mortals to know every aspect of the universe and how God manages "worlds without number" (Moses 1:33). Even the revered prophet Moses only received revelation "of this earth, and the inhabitants thereof" (v. 35). Under God's divine authority, scientific discoveries and the laws of the universe all combine together with gospel principles and make one great whole of truth.

> After all truth is gathered into one great body of information, the questions of the physical and social scientists will be answered. Modern prophets, such as Joseph Smith and Joseph F. Smith, have declared that eventually all truth will be circumscribed into one great whole, with the laws of the universe and the gospel unified together. As one small, but important, example of this, in the twentieth century, Albert Einstein concluded scientifically what the Prophet Joseph Smith had taught doctrinally in the nineteenth century: matter can be neither created nor destroyed, but merely changed from one form to another. Einstein's discovery of relativity between matter and energy in the physical world revolutionized modern science, just as the Prophet's revelations on the eternal nature of elements in the human spirit transformed traditional Christian ideas about man's creation and progression. [Victor Ludlow, *Principles and Practices of the Restored Gospel*, 139.]

Laws of Nature

Besides searching the scriptures to enhance our spiritual knowledge and studying temporal sources to enrich our general understanding of the world, we can also learn about our Creator by observing His creations. An old folk song states, "This land is made for you and me." A more complete rendering is. "This *world* is made for you and me." Our loving Heavenly Father, through His Beloved Son, created the beauties of nature for our enjoyment and rejoicing. Everywhere we look, from tiny dewdrops on rosebuds to vast oceans filled with unusual creatures, from snow-flocked Himalayan peaks to the deepest desert valleys, "all things are made to bear record of [God]" (Moses 6:63). The Light of Christ dwells within every form of life—all flora and fauna—from the tiniest plankton or amoeba to the most complex human being.

A few summers ago while camping at Yosemite National Park, I discovered several reminders of our Creator. Yosemite's monolithic rock formations take one's breath away with their magnificence, symbolizing that Christ is the "Messiah, the King of Zion, the Rock of Heaven, which is broad as eternity" (Moses 7:53). It's impossible to fall off a rock as broad as eternity. "Remember, remember that it is upon the rock of our Redeemer, who is Christ, the Son of God, that ye must build your foundation;… the rock upon which ye are built, which is a sure foundation, a foundation where if men build they cannot fall" (Helaman 5:12).

In the protected areas of the National Park, the waters were so clear and clean I could see stones and moss at the bottom of every stream, river, and lake. That prompts me to purify my life by partaking of the living water Jesus offers.

I especially enjoy hiking on trails where tall pines stretch to the sky. Even if a treetop has been lopped off in a storm, one of the upper pine bows will twist its way around until it becomes the pinnacle pointing heavenward. Also, if a tree has been bent sideways by heavy rocks or snowfall, the arch in the trunk may remain, but it will again curve and grow upward toward the light. In a similar sense, if I make mistakes that weigh me down, I can overcome them through repentance and by looking upward to Christ.

On wintry days when I ski or snowshoe, the pine boughs are often laden with mounds of newly-fallen snow. Later, as the sun bursts from behind the clouds and warms the earth, melting begins, then the snow takes a sudden slide off the boughs and plops to the ground. I'm reminded that the burdens I carry can be overcome by relying on the Son of God World, who said, "Come unto me, all ye that labor and are heavy laden, and I will give you rest" (Matthew 11:28).

More than once I've been doused by a falling clump of snow, but it's usually minor compared to the showers that spray me while skiing through powder. In deep snow on the ski slopes, eventually I will fall or do a face plant in a mound of white. Then I must dig myself and my skis out of the powder, and wipe snow from my collar, pockets, and cuffs. Brrr.

I recall a day of digging our daughter Erin out of a worse situation. Glenn and I had taken her Erin to cross country ski on the snow-packed road to Smith and Morehouse Reservoir. When we reached the boat dock, which sloped down to the ice-covered water, Erin thought it would be delightful to ski down the ramp and out across the frozen lake. So down she zoomed while Glenn and I watched. When Erin reached the edge of the lake, rather than proceeding across the ice, she suddenly came to a halt. Then we saw her tugging and jerking her legs, trying to move. But she was going nowhere. Finally, she hollered for help.

When Glenn and I skied down the ramp to join her, we quickly saw the problem. Instead of a smooth transition from the snowy ramp to the frozen lake, there was a three-inch gap of water—just enough for Erin's skis to fit beneath the ice and get wedged. Being a mother, I said in jest, "Stupid is as stupid does!"

Actually Erin is far from stupid, for she's employed as an aerospace engineer—otherwise known as a rocket scientist. But, as many of us do, she made a mistake. Thankfully, it was something we could laugh about as she took off her skis and the three of us wrestled them from beneath the icy layer. We then discovered the air was cold enough that the water froze instantly on her skis, and we spent ten minutes scraping them off so we could continue our skiing.

Most of us are grateful to have support from others if we get stuck in tough circumstances. But in the trek toward salvation, the most reliable source of assistance is Jesus Christ. Why try to go it alone when the Lord is nearby to assist us? Whether we're troubled by cares of the world or struggling to learn eternal truth, our Savior can rescue us if we ask for His help.

Truth Abides Forever

We are nothing without Christ, whose "truth abideth forever and ever" (D&C 1:39). As King Benjamin said, "always retain in remembrance, the greatness of God, and your own nothingness, and his goodness and long-suffering towards you, unworthy creatures, and humble yourselves even in the depths of humility, calling on the name of the Lord daily, and standing steadfastly in the faith of that which is to come" (Mosiah 4:11). We are further encouraged to "Stand therefore, having your loins girt about with truth, having on the breastplate of righteousness,... Taking the shield of faith wherewith ye shall be able to quench all the fiery darts of the wicked" (D&C 27:16–17, see also Ephesians 6:14–17).

Opposing Satan and his fiery darts seems to be a daily battle. Yet when we stand firmly in righteousness, protected by truth and faith, we can successfully wield off any devilish dart—fiery or not—real or imagined.

As the lone Nephite survivor, the Prophet Moroni did more than his share of quenching darts, while the entire nation of Lamanites sought to destroy him. Both a fearless soldier and prophet of God, Moroni provided the formula to know the truth of all things.

> And when ye shall receive these things, I would exhort you that ye would ask God, the Eternal Father, in the name of Christ, if these things are not true; and if ye shall ask with a sincere heart, with real intent, having faith in Christ, he will manifest the truth of it unto you, by the power of the Holy Ghost.
>
> And by the power of the Holy Ghost ye may know the truth of all things. (Moroni 10:4–5)

The Holy Ghost is a bearer and witness of truth. Thus, we must constantly strive to be worthy of His influence in our lives. There's no sense in pretending to be righteous. Endeavoring to perform sleight of hand magic tricks will not be effective. Executing a Houdini-like feat of illusion will be frowned upon. Our Father can look "down upon all the children of men; and he knows all the thoughts and intents of the heart; for by his hand were they all created from the beginning" (Alma 18:32).

I am awestruck to know that God's limitless intellect can simultaneously view the past, present, and future. "The angels do not reside on a planet like this earth; But they reside in the presence of God, on a globe like a sea of glass and fire, where all things for their glory are manifest, past, present, and future, and are continually before the Lord" (D&C 130: 6–7).

Imagine possessing the phenomenal gift of seeing everyone's life—past, present, and future! It would be like viewing the movies "Ben Hur," "Back to the Future" and "Star Wars" all at once. My head reels at the thought of so many movie reels—like something straight from "The Twilight Zone." Is it any wonder that Nephi praised God for His knowledge of all things? "O how great the holiness of our God! For he knoweth all things and there is not anything save he knows it" (2 Nephi 9:20). How vast are the truths we've received, and still there are many yet to be revealed to us! "Truth is knowledge of things as they are, and as they were, and as they are to come;... He that keepeth his commandments receiveth truth and light, until he is glorified in truth and knoweth all things" (D&C 93:24, 28).

Prophecies foretell a day when we'll obtain the sealed scriptures and historical records of all people who have lived on earth. Perhaps we haven't yet received them because our mortal minds aren't capable of comprehending such measureless knowledge. I wonder when that time will come. Of course, that's the key: *time*. In some future day, time, as we know, it will not exist. How I long for that day! Then I'll never be late again! No more deadlines to meet. I can double schedule appointments on my calendar. The stress of frantic freeway driving will disappear. Wow! That's something to look forward to! Just one of the perks of eternal life, I suppose.

How glorious that the Father and Son make their immeasurable knowledge available to us! Though it may take eternity to become fully enlightened, truth is available, now and forever, to those who earnestly seek it. As King Benjamin counseled, "you should... open your ears that ye may hear, and your hearts that ye may understand, and your minds that the mysteries of God may be unfolded to your view" (Mosiah 2:9).

Christ is the Light of Truth

Christ is present in all the world, for He is "in all and through all things, the light of truth" (D&C 88:6). Wherever I go, I enjoy observing people—children, teenagers, adults, foreigners, newlyweds, soldiers, sailors, civilians, politicians, mothers, fathers, grandparents, Christians, Jews, Muslims—in all walks of life. Within every living soul is a spark of divinity, for each is the spiritual offspring of our Father in Heaven. The Light of Christ is "the true Light which lighteth every man that cometh into the world" (John 1:9). The "Spirit of Christ" guides us to "know good from evil" (Moroni 7:16). However, that influence can weaken, diminish, and nearly vanish when evil is repeatedly chosen over good.

At the genesis of the world, our Father created all things through the workmanship of His Son. Then He declared, "And I, God, saw everything that I had made, and, behold, all things which I had made were very good" (Moses 2:31). That means every human is inherently good. How sad that millions and billions of our Father's children are "only kept from the truth because they know not where to find it" (D&C 123:12). What a responsibility for Latter-day Saints to hold up the Light of Christ that His eternal truth might permeate every living soul!

The Christmas season abounds in colorful lights to celebrate the birth of Jesus Christ, the Light of the World. Living in downtown Salt Lake City, I'm privileged to frequently see the array of lights at Temple Square. Last Christmas when my son brought his family to visit during the holidays, we bundled up in warm clothing and strolled through the temple grounds.

In the midst of the block we stopped to view the life-sized nativity, with the accompanying narration of Jesus' birth. I sat on a stone bench, while my rambunctious four-year-old grandson stood beside me, listening to the nativity story with its interspersed music. Knowing that he rarely holds still, I wrapped an arm around his waist so he wouldn't fall off the bench. I was amazed at how quiet he remained during the scriptural account, while spotlights splayed from the stable with Mary, Joseph, and baby Jesus, to the shepherds, then the wise men. At the end of the brief broadcast came the voice of President Hinckley, followed by a hymn from the Tabernacle Choir. Then an enormous light beamed up from the stable where baby Jesus slept. It stretched toward the skies as far as the eye could see. I whispered to my grandson, "See how that light goes all the way toward heaven?"

He nodded and said with enthusiasm, "I wish I could climb up that light and see our Savior!"

How sweet, yet stunning, was his childlike faith! It made me also wish I could climb up that light and see our Savior, who is "the light, and the life, and the truth of the world" (Ether 4:12).

Be True to the Truth

Sadly, there are some who once walked the path of truth in The Church of Jesus Christ of Latter-day Saints, but who have allowed themselves to be blown astray by the "wisdom of the world," which "is foolishness with God" (1 Corinthians 3:19). Scarcely any stake or district of the Church is not without dissenters, who ofttimes stir up contention.

I met with such opposition in the spring of 1990. Because of my love of the outdoors, I signed up for an evening class, "Women and Nature." Not only did the title of this class at the University of Utah intrigue me, but also its instructor. I had previously read some of her books, and I'd heard her speak a few times. On the first evening of class, she introduced herself, giving her name, then saying, "I am a Mormon—not orthodox—but that is my roots." It's strange that any instructor at any university would deem it important to mention a background of unorthodox Mormonism. As the weeks ensued, I discovered that though she claimed Mormon roots, the path she followed veered far from a pious point of view.

I had assumed we would focus on women enjoying nature, but instead, the course was steeped in a metaphysical realm, the "nature of women." Forty people—only one male—had registered for the class. They were of varying ages and classifications. During each three-hour session, I found many of the topics to be offensive: goddess worship, flaunting our sexuality, rituals to honor our bodies, taking upon us a token animal, retaliating with rage against our patriarchal society, tapping into our hidden feminine powers as a witch does, and to top it off, one evening we drove into the mountains to hold a moon ritual.

Most *sensible* LDS women would have dropped the class. But not me, the risk taker! Despite danger signals blaring inside me, I thought I could withstand any blows to my character and my testimony of the gospel. Beyond that, I was dumb enough to believe that my maintaining a vibrant LDS stand would positively influence others in the class. Besides, it was merely a twelve-week quarter at the university, then it would end. Thank goodness it wasn't any longer, or I might have gone overboard into deep water.

One requirement was that we keep a journal of thoughts and feelings about whatever we discussed or read for class. My journal contained many scriptural quotes and my own gospel-based thoughts to counteract the dreadful topics. Four weeks into the quarter, the instructor gathered up our journals to read them. After that, she honed into my strict LDS perspective and began to purposely call on me to share my opinion. Her desire was that my words would provoke a debate in the classroom—which often occurred. Each time I shared my conservative, religious thoughts, forty pairs of eyes scowled at me. But I kept my integrity and spoke without shame for my faith. Never once did I evade making an honest response, nor did I skip attending the class.

Halfway through the quarter, we discussed a disgusting book, which flagrantly upset my value system. I won't divulge the book's title, nor it's subject, because I prefer to protect my readers from this shameful matter. Looking back, I can't believe I read the book to the very end. I'm not proud to admit it. As usual, that night our instructor asked me to express my feelings, which I did, citing the religious beliefs I hold dear. In my view, accepting immoral and atrocious behavior is the cause of much needless suffering in the world: broken marriages, failed families, warfare, disease, drugs, and so on. Of course, at this university's level of liberal permissiveness, my comments lit a fire of explosive words from other class members. I couldn't wait for the session to end.

The next week I slumped into my chair to endure a slightly-less caustic topic about taking care of Mother Earth. Our radical instructor claimed that our patriarchal society was harming the earth's environment, and it was our duty as women to revolt in rage and let our voices be heard. She gave a personal account of her recent protesting in southern Utah where ranchers had dragged chains to rip out trees and make grazing areas for their cattle. She also described an earlier demonstration at the Nevada nuclear test sites, acting proud of herself for being arrested and jailed for her actions. In our class that night, most of the students agreed that it's acceptable to protest in rage against society's crudities to Mother Earth.

I tried to remain silent, though I felt rage is rarely justified. I'd been taught, not only by religion but also by society, to promote positive actions—to be part of the solution rather than accelerating the problem. When our instructor called upon me to speak, I said that passionate rage is not the answer to events that are already controversial. I believed that opposition expressed in a quiet manner was often more effective and had longer lasting results. My comments made no impact on my classmates, who rolled their eyes and gnashed their teeth against society's seeming injustices.

During the usual ten-minute break in the midst of the three-hour course, our instructor came to ask if I'd stay after and talk with her. I said I would, hoping that my odds would be better one-on-one with her than against the entire class. After all, she did profess to be LDS.

As the next hour ended and students began to retreat from the room, I stayed in my seat. I soon discovered that our instructor had also asked three other women to remain. She gathered us into a small circle of chairs, then started our chat by saying, "Bonnie, these are the other Mormon women from our class." I knew one of them as her cousin, one as a husky masculine woman, and the third as a tender-hearted 22-year-old student. I'd paid particular attention to this young woman, for I watched her be swayed in our classes from her humble Mormon moorings to a more worldly view. The other two women—the instructor's cousin and the masculine woman—had made enough comments in class to let me know they'd long ago lost their religious fervor.

Alone I sat—in the hot seat—facing the four of them. Our instructor recapped the last week's chatter about the book I'd objected to, then she and her "three musketeers" attempted to rescue me from my orthodox ways. Their goal was to convince me that the book was merely symbolic of our need to get in touch with our wild side—that as women we had the right to delve into the dark things in life. I maintained my stand that darkness derived from Satan, and we must "abstain from all appearance of evil" (1 Thessalonians 5:22).

Frequently reminding me that they, too, were Mormons, the discussion turned to the need for strong women to exhibit rage, exposing the defects in our patriarchal society and religion. For over an hour I endured their badgering me with unrighteous perspectives—though I was grateful the young student said very little.

For the first while, I felt sorry for myself, with the unwarranted harassment leveled upon me. But after a time, I forgot my own discomfort and began to ache for these women. They were my sisters in the gospel, yet they were caught in the snares of Satan. Though unseen to the naked eye, the fetters and chains of darkness weighed them down, contaminating their faith in Christ. These were precious daughters of our Heavenly Father, yet they didn't think it important to remain pure and holy before Him. I began to see these four women not as Musketeers, but as Mouseketeers. They'd allowed their divine spirits to diminish, vanquishing the Light of Christ that once dwelt within them. Now they were tiny and weak and had become prey to Satan's mousetraps.

When finally we finished our conversation that evening, I was emotionally drained and spiritually exhausted. My fatigue came partly from the vigorous effort to protect my faith, but I was more drained from the burden of pain I felt for these four women. They'd hardened their hearts against the truth and chosen darkness instead of light (see Helaman 13:29).

As soon as we finished, I rushed from the building and climbed into my car. Tears cascaded down my face, and, with deep sobs, I prayed for peace to return to my soul. With the extraordinary sorrow I felt for these woman, I knew our Father also grieved for them, and for all His misled children.

Even after that tormenting night, I stuck it out through the last few weeks of class. For the final exam of essay questions, our instructor said we could quote from any source to make our point. One essay question asked how we might ease the pain that mankind inflicts upon Mother Earth. I referenced Moses 7, when "Enoch wept and cried unto the Lord, saying: When shall the earth rest?" (v. 58)

> And it came to pass that Enoch looked upon the earth; and he heard a voice from the bowels thereof, saying: Wo, wo is me, the mother of men; I am pained, I am weary, because of the wickedness of my children. When shall I rest, and be cleansed from the filthiness which is gone forth out of me? When will my Creator sanctify me, that I may rest, and righteousness for a season abide upon my face?
>
> And when Enoch heard the earth mourn, he wept, and cried unto the Lord, saying: O Lord, wilt thou not have compassion upon the earth? (Moses 7:48–49)

Though in my essay I agreed that Mother Earth does deserve a rest, it's not because of environmental issues, but rather, that our world must be freed from the darkness and wickedness which bedevil humankind. It seems, however, my written words touched a sensitive nerve when my instructor read them. Receiving the exam back, I found she had crossed out that essay and totally disallowed my use of scripture, though previously she'd said we could use any source. As a result, I received only a "B," in the class, despite completing all the requirements and having perfect attendance with frequent participation in the discussions. But my grade doesn't matter in an eternal perspective—only that I stayed true to the truth. Through that experience, I knew with surety that adhering to truth can repel iniquity, for "Light and truth forsake that evil one" (D&C 93:37).

So there you have it. I learned the importance of being an exhibitionist—not by taking off my clothes, but by the opposite—by putting on a mantle of truth, taking upon myself the name of Christ, and wearing the uniform of a child of God. Have you ever realized that our Father provides better employee compensation packages and retirement benefits than any earthly employer? All we must do is cleave to the truth and allow His Spirit to work miracles within us.

Once we have received "the word of truth... by the Spirit of truth" (D&C 50:19), we are asked to "preach the word of truth by the Comforter, in the Spirit of truth" (v. 17). Although I did not learn what I'd expected to study in that university class, the experience enhanced my faith and closeness with the Lord. I testify that the Spirit of God upheld me while I stood alone to champion the truths I hold dear. I know He will do the same for you.

Grow in Grace and Truth

It may seem difficult to defend the truth when confronted by mockery and scorn, but that is how we become better children of God. "Behold, ye are little children and ye cannot bear all things now; ye must grow in grace and in the knowledge of the truth" (D&C 50:40). Just as our physical bodies mature from childhood to adulthood, our spirits also must develop gradually toward godhood. At the age of fourteen, the Prophet Joseph Smith was frequently persecuted for telling this truth. Yet he maintained his integrity:

> I had actually seen a light, and in the midst of that light I saw two Personages, and they did in reality speak to me; and though I was hated and persecuted for saying that I had seen a vision, yet was true;... Why persecute me for telling the truth? I have actually seen a vision; and who am I that I can withstand God, or why does the world think to make me deny what I have actually seen? For I had seen a vision; I knew it,

and I knew that God knew it, and I could not deny it, neither dared I do it; at least I knew that by so doing I would offend God, and come under condemnation (Joseph Smith History 1:25).

During that tumultuous university class, I more clearly understood Joseph's words. I had a testimony that God lives and that Jesus atoned for the sins of the world. Through the Holy Ghost, the Lord had revealed many truths to me, and I was obligated to share what I knew, for God knew that I knew. Though there were times I wanted to do a disappearing act from class, I endured to the end and was blessed for my efforts.

> When one knows what is right one should always have the courage to defend it even in the face of ridicule or punishment.
> The Prophet Joseph, for example, was reviled and persecuted for saying that he had received a vision, but he always remained true to his testimony. [David O. McKay, *Ancient Apostles*, Deseret Book Co., Salt Lake City, 1964, 185, paragraphing altered.]

Despite encountering much opposition, from his boyhood until his untimely martyrdom, Joseph Smith continued to impart truths of the gospel. He wrote the following words to encourage each of us to uphold the standard of truth.

> The standard of truth has been erected; no unhallowed hand can stop the work from progressing, persecutions may rage, mobs may combine, armies may assemble, calumny may defame, but the truth of God will go forth boldly, nobly, and independent, till it has penetrated every continent, visited every clime, swept every country, and sounded in every ear, till the purposes of God shall be accomplished and the great Jehovah shall say the work is done. [Joseph Smith, *History of the Church* 4:54.]

Conclusion

How blessed we are to know our Father in Heaven and Jesus Christ have fully restored the truths of the gospel in these latter-days! As righteousness increases, more magnificent revelations will come to light prior to the Second Coming of the Lord. Truth will flood the earth, for God has promised, "righteousness will I send down out of heaven; and truth will I send forth out of the earth, to bear testimony of mine Only Begotten;… and righteousness and truth will I cause to sweep the earth as with a flood, to gather out mine elect from the four quarters of the earth, unto a place which I shall prepare, an Holy City" (Moses 7:62).

Only righteous individuals will be welcomed within the walls of that Holy City. Spirituality is not sold in vending machines. Nor can eternal truth be derived from fortune tellers with crystal balls. How blessed we are to have a living prophet, who reveals truth directly from God! Yet there are still billions of people without access to the truth of their divine origin—so few who know they are literally the seed of Deity. Each needs to be taught that "redemption cometh in and through the Holy Messiah, who is full of grace and truth" (2 Nephi 2:6).

> Standing upon its broad platform, encircled by the mantle of truth, the man of God, by faith, peers into the future, withdraws the curtains of eternity, unveils the mystery of the heavens, and through the dark vista of unnumbered years, beholds the purposes of the great Elohim, as they roll forth in all their majesty and power and glory. Thus standing upon a narrow neck of space, and beholding the past, present, and the future, he sees himself an eternal being claiming an affinity with God, a son of God, a spark of Deity struck from the fire of his eternal blaze. He looks upon the world and man, in all their various phases, knows his true interests, and with intelligence imparted by his Father Celestial, he comprehends their origin and destiny.…

His intelligence, lit up by God and followed out, will be expansive as the world and spread through space; his law is the law of love; his rule, the rule of right to all. He loves his neighbor, and he does him good; he loves his God and therefore worships him; he sees the power of truth, which, like the light of God, spreads through all space, illuminates all worlds, and penetrates where men or angels, God or spheres are known; he clings to it. Truth is his helmet, buckler, shield, his rock, defense; his all in time and in eternity.... He grasps at all truths, human and divine.... He has nothing to lose but error, and nothing to gain but truth. He digs, labors, and searches for it as for hidden treasure; and while others are content with chaff and husks of straw, he seizes on the kernel, substance, the gist of all that's good, and clings to all that will ennoble and exalt the human family....

Did ancient men of God revel in truth? So do we. [John Taylor, *Teachings of the Presidents of the Church: John Taylor*, 211–212.]

Those who revel in truth—daily, hourly, and minute by minute—will be centered in Christ, who is "in all and through all things, the light of truth; Which truth shineth. This is the light of Christ" (D&C 88:6–77).

For additional insight see:
Doctrine and Covenants, sections 88 and 93.
Victor Ludlow, *Principles and Practices of the Restored Gospel*, Deseret Book Co., Salt Lake City, 1992.
John A. Widstoe, "The Acceptance of all Truth," *Improvement Era*, 1938.
John Taylor, *Teachings of the Presidents of the Church*, 2001, 211–212.

I am the resurrection, and the life:
he that believeth in me, though he were dead,
yet shall he live;
John 11:25

The Resurrection and the Life

At a time when Martha grieved with her sister, Mary, over the death of their brother Lazarus, "Jesus said unto her, I am the resurrection, and the life: he that believeth in me, though he were dead, yet shall he live" (John 11:25). Trusting in Jesus was a comfort to Martha and Mary, as it can be to anyone facing trials. Death becomes inconsequential with hope and faith in the resurrection and Atonement of Christ.

The Savior has shown us the pathway that leads us home to live with our Father eternally. His "way is perfect" (2 Samuel 22:31), for "he cannot walk in crooked paths; neither doth he vary from that which he hath said;... therefore his course is one eternal round" (Alma 7:20). He is "Wonderful, Counsellor, The mighty God, The everlasting Father, The Prince of Peace" (Isaiah 9:6). Lovingly He gathers His sheep as the "Good Shepherd" (John 10:11, 14), for "the Lord Omnipotent... reigneth,... from all eternity to all eternity." With unselfish, unfathomable love, Jesus let soldiers nail Him to the cross. With almighty, omnipotent love, God the Father allowed His Beloved Son to die.

Jesus and His Atonement represent the most profound expression of Heavenly Father's love for His children. How important the free gift of the resurrection is for all mankind and the proffer of the greatest gift which even God can give, eternal life to those willing to so live and to so qualify. [Neal A. Maxwell, August 29, 1999 Missionary Satellite Broadcast, reported in *Church News*, Sept. 4, 1999, 5.]

God's love is miraculous, unchanging, empowering, and everlasting. "God is love; and he that dwelleth in love dwelleth in God, and God in him" (1 John 4:16). Imagine dwelling eternally enveloped in celestial love with the Father and the Son! No wonder "eternal life... is the greatest of all the gifts of God" (D&C 14:7).

To consider the opposite course, eternal damnation, is frightening, yet "it must needs be that there was an opposition; even the forbidden fruit in opposition to the tree of life; the one being sweet and the other bitter. Wherefore, the Lord God gave unto man that he should act for himself. Wherefore, man could not act for himself save it should be that he was enticed by the one or the other" (2 Nephi 2:15–16).

As a twelve-year-old, I experienced something akin to meeting Satan. Each weekday, I walked with a friend to junior high school, which was outside our familiar and secure neighborhood. One building we passed each day was a halfway house for mentally ill men. Looking back now as an adult, I know these men must have been harmless, or they would not have been allowed to go outside. Yet I shall never forget the shivery feeling on one autumn morning as my friend and I passed this house.

Several men were in the yard, but our attention was riveted on brawny man, who stood on the grassy parking strip between the sidewalk and the street. He carried a hefty pick over his shoulder, as if he were working in a mine. At the exact moment my friend and I passed by him, he raised the pick high in the air then slammed it with vengeance into the ground. My friend and I took off running—both of us sure that we were his next targets. Even after we reached the school, my heart continued to throb with fear. Thereafter, my friend and I walked across the street to keep a safe distance from the man with the pick, who frequently stood in the yard. He might as well have been Satan, for that's what my adolescent mind conjured up. That frightening moment reminds me to keep a safe distance from the devil and his unpredictable tactics. Only by staying on a righteous pathway can I have a chance at exaltation in the celestial kingdom.

The glories of eternal life are vastly beyond anything we may have witnessed on earth or imagined in our hearts—more spectacular than Fourth of July fireworks, the opening ceremonies before the Olympics, or a combination of all the sunrises and sunsets ever seen. Perhaps we'll need sunglasses to shade us from the magnificent radiance of Christ and the majestic glory of God the Father. No doubt our frames will quake, and we will fall upon our knees before Them. Yet the Father and Son are without pride, and neither of Them will want us to remain in a worshipful posture before Their thrones. They will bid us to arise and move ahead toward resplendent blessings as we continue to serve, learn, and love throughout eternity.

Greater Love Hath No Man

Jesus offered us love beyond human comprehension. Pure and perfect love requires tremendous sacrifice, which He demonstrated on the cross. "Greater love hath no man than this, that a man lay down his life for his friends" (John 15:13).

We see this type of selfless love in a father who enters a burning house to save his children, in a mother risking her own health to bring forth a child, in a brother or sister who donates a kidney for a sibling, or in soldiers going to battle to provide liberty for others. Recently an e-mail circulated saying that Americans live in "the land of the free, because of the brave." Bravery is essential in offering one's life to save another. Love is also indispensable.

The pure love of Christ is undeniably the highest expression of love. In order to cultivate this gift, we must pray "with all the energy of heart, that [we] may be filled with this love" (Moroni 7:48).

None of God's children, not even Jesus, was sent to earth with a full comprehension of how to perform our Father's work. Not until "Jesus himself began to be about thirty years of age" (Luke 3:23), was He eligible to serve as a Jewish rabbi or preacher (see Numbers 4:3). He did not prepare overnight for this holy ministry. As a boy, He not only studied religious tenets of the day, but He also communed with Father in Heaven in a very direct way. As an adult, Jesus fasted and prayed to God for forty days in the wilderness, where He also rebuffed Satan. Only in a gradual manner did the Savior prepare Himself for the sacrifice that would "bring redemption to the world, to save the world from sin" (3 Nephi 9:21).

As with all of God's children, Jesus had to increase in spiritual knowledge "line upon line, precept upon precept" (D&C 98:12). It took thirty-three years before He attained the characteristics of godliness to perform the Father's will. If anyone else claims they could achieve what Christ did in such a short span of time, I would say, "Liar, liar, pants on fire!"

We often focus on how Jesus suffered for the sins of the world, but His Atonement also covered our "pains and afflictions and temptations of every kind." He absorbed "the pains and sicknesses of his people" and he took "upon him death,... [and] their infirmities, that his bowels may be filled with mercy" (Alma 7:11–12).

Verse 13 adds, "Now the Spirit knoweth all things; nevertheless the Son of God suffereth according to the flesh." In other words, Jesus could have known through the Spirit how it would feel to bear these burdens. But instead of using His spiritual intuition, He chose to feel these things first-hand through His suffering in the flesh. In a way incomprehensible to mere mortals, Jesus "hath borne our griefs, and carried our sorrows" (Isaiah 53:4).

Jesus did not wait until Gethsemane or Calvary to shoulder all these afflictions. In His daily walks through Palestine, Jesus practiced using His divine power on one individual after another. Consider the "woman which had a spirit of infirmity eighteen years, and was bowed together, and could in no wise lift up herself." After calling her to come unto him, Jesus said, "Woman, thou art loosed from thine infirmity." Then laying "his hands on her ... *immediately* she was made straight, and glorified God" (Luke 13:11–13, italics added).

Immediately she was healed. She didn't have to await Christ's crucifixion for Him to take away her infirmity. From the very beginning of His ministry, Jesus used His divine power to instantly bless people's lives. Whether lame, blind, leprous, deaf, or possessed by evil spirits, "there went virtue out of him, and he healed them all" (Luke 6:19).

Power on Earth

With His divine investiture, Jesus freed people from their sins without causing them to await His Atonement. One example was on a day within a crowded house, wherein people lowered a man with palsy through the roof. "Jesus seeing their faith said unto the sick of the palsy; Son, be of good cheer; thy sins be forgiven thee" (Matthew 9:2). Utilizing His "power on earth to forgive sins" (v. 6), Jesus immediately brought this man relief from suffering.

One small miraculous step at a time, Jesus liberated many from their pain, grief, illness, and iniquity. Our Redeemer brought salvation—in both physical and spiritual ways—to those who had faith to receive it. This was part of Christ's training and preparation for bearing all the sins and sorrows of the world on the horrendous day of atonement. In addition to restoring health and casting out devils, Jesus performed miracles in raising at least three people from their deathbeds. All this He did prior to the cross, where He took death upon himself "that he may loose the bands of death which bind his people" (Alma 7:12).

The first instance of Christ restoring life was when the ruler of the synagogue, Jairus, "fell down at Jesus' feet, and besought him that he would come" heal his "only daughter, about twelve years of age, and she lay a dying" (Luke 8:41–42). But there was a delay as people thronged the Master—including the woman with an issue of blood, who was healed by touching Christ's clothes. Then there came a report from the house of Jairus, saying, "Thy daughter is dead; trouble not the Master" (v. 49). Yet Jesus overheard the news, and said, "Fear not: believe only, and she shall be made whole" (v. 50). Soon Jesus arrived at the scene, where many wept and bewailed the girl's death.

> But he said, Weep not; she is not dead, but sleepeth.
>
> And they laughed him to scorn, knowing that she was dead.
>
> And he put them all out, and took her by the hand, and called, saying, Maid, arise.
>
> And her spirit came again, and she arose straightway: and he commanded to give her meat.
>
> And her parents were astonished: but he charged them that they should tell no man what was done (Luke 8:52–56).

This damsel had but barely died while Jesus made his way to her bedside. Her arising was nonetheless a miracle, which awed those who mourned and wept. Another scripture records how Jesus used His developing power to bless a man who had been dead long enough that his body was carried forth to the burial.

> Now when [Jesus] came nigh to the gate of the city [Nain], behold, there was a dead man carried out, the only son of his mother, and she was a widow: and much people of the city was with her.
>
> And when the Lord saw her, he had compassion on her, and said unto her, Weep not.
>
> And he came and touched the bier: and they that bare him stood still. And he said, Young man, I say unto thee, Arise.
>
> And he that was dead sat up, and began to speak. And he delivered him to his mother.
>
> And there came a fear on all: and they glorified God, saying, That a great prophet is risen up among us; and, That God hath visited his people (Luke 7:11–16).

Though the people of Nain witnessed this manifestation of God's power on earth, many still did not grasp that it was the Son of God who wrought the miracle. Nor did they realize that this phenomenal event enhanced Christ's comprehension of what He would face on the cross of Calvary.

Jesus further prepared for the atonement by the more astonishing miracle of raising Lazarus from the tomb. As a dear friend to Lazarus, Jesus was saddened by the report that he was sick enough to die and needed a blessing. Yet the Lord waited to go unto him until the fourth day after Lazarus' entombment, when Jewish people believed the spirit separated from the body. With previous experience releasing the chains of death, Christ displayed stunning majesty as He called Lazarus forth from the stony tomb and restored him to life (see John 11:11–46). This miracle further prepared Jesus for the time when His own body would be laid in a tomb, and then arise on the third day in glorious resurrection.

Although Jesus brought the daughter of Jairus, the man from Nain, and Lazarus back to life, this did not constitute a resurrection, for these three would still face mortal death. No one could partake in resurrection until after "the resurrection of Christ from the dead" (Alma 40:15).

Each time Jesus restored health or life to individuals on earth, He increased in comprehension of how to bear pain, sicknesses, and infirmities. He also knew how to victoriously overcome death. These events prepared Him for the all-consuming sacrifice of the Atonement, which would cover every sin and pain in the world. Christ's promise will forever remain, "I shall heal them" (3 Nephi 18:32).

This Is My Beloved Son

The transfiguration also prepared Jesus to be the resurrection and the life of the world. Peter, James, and John went with Him to a mountain away from the people. They witnessed as "his face did shine as the sun, and his raiment was white as the light" (Matthew 17:2), for "the fashion of his countenance was altered, and his raiment was white and glistering" (Luke 9:29). Though Peter, James, and John had seen many heaven-sent miracles, nothing compared to this dazzling display. Imagine their astonishment when "there appeared unto them Elias with Moses: and they were talking with Jesus" (Mark 9:4). Then came the supreme moment when "a bright cloud overshadowed them: and behold a voice out of the cloud, which said, This is my beloved Son, in whom I am well pleased; hear ye him" (Matthew 17:5). Is it any wonder that "when the disciples heard it, they fell on their face, and were sore afraid" (v. 6)? The voice of God the Father is so rarely heard that anyone would be stunned, especially while enveloped in a bright cloud, which meant God's presence was near.

These three apostles were so afraid they had fallen to the ground in fear. Picture the brawny fisherman, Simon Peter, whose name means stone or rock, trembling like a frightened child with his face buried in his hands. James and John also cowered in fear beside him. Then in a tender way, "Jesus came and touched them, and said, Arise, and be not afraid." The visual imagery in this scene is dramatic. Jesus mercifully reached forth, touched Peter, James, and John, then soothed them with the words, "Arise and be not afraid." Surely they felt His tranquil, healing power at that moment.

Whenever we cringe and hide while faced with unexplainable circumstances, or if we fall on our knees with doubtful hearts, Jesus can touch our lives and bid us to "arise and be not afraid."

The next verse is also thought-provoking, for "when they had lifted up their eyes, they saw no man, save Jesus only" (Matthew 17:8). All of us, like these three disciples, are blessed when we keep our focus on Jesus—and no one else. The more we center our thoughts on Christ, the more our fears will dissipate. Then we can arise from our knees with greater faith and confidence to overcome whatever we confront in life. I testify that this is a true principle.

Though these three disciples were devout and committed to the gospel, they still had moments of doubt and fear—just as our faith and trust in God waver from time to time. It's like walking a tightrope—not that I have experience in tightropes: sometimes we lean toward the side of worldliness rather than walking a straight line to heaven. That's when we must readjust our grip on the balance beam to gain equilibrium. If we always remember the wooden beam Jesus carried toward Calvary, we're more likely to stay the course and be true to the gospel covenants we've made. Then we can receive "the peace of God, which passeth all understanding" (Philippians 4:7). Each child of God can discover that peace is not simply the absence of conflict in our lives, but that true peace is living in harmony with Deity.

Zion, the Pure in Heart

Zion is synonymous with the kingdom of heaven, where God and Christ dwell. Only those with charity, "the pure love of Christ" (Moroni 7:47), will be welcomed within the celestial gates.

There are days I need a tangible reminder to share the pure love of Christ with everyone around me—something like my old mood ring with the stone that turned different colors when I was angry or stressed. But even a mood ring can be moody and unreliable. When I put the ring on my stuffed monkey, who never gets irritated or annoyed, the stone changed colors according to temperature and air pressure.

That makes me think. What if we had barometers in every house and building—not to measure air pressure but to calculate the degree of charity and love in a room? What if you could invent such an item and sell it all over the world? But I doubt it would be a "get rich quick" scheme, because lots of folks still aren't sure what charity, the pure love of Christ, really is.

A community founded upon pure love is rarely achieved. Though Enoch and his people attained it, this miracle did not occur within a brief span of time. Because of Enoch's faith, he could preach with such divine power that he caused the earth to tremble, rivers to divert their paths, and mountains to move. Thus, only righteous individuals dared to join his flock, while "so great was the fear of the enemies of the people of God, that they fled" (Moses 7:14).

And it came to pass that Enoch talked with the Lord; and he said unto the Lord: Surely Zion shall dwell in safety forever.

But the Lord said unto Enoch: Zion have I blessed, but the residue of the people have I cursed (Moses 7:20).

God blessed His children in Zion, but cursed the "residue of the people." What kind of image comes to mind with the word *residue*? Scraps left after a bounteous feast? Floating debris in a lake? Small remnants of unusable fabric? Contents of a trash dumpster? Now compare those images to the inhabitants of earth as residue. Rather caustic, don't you think? So, which would you choose: to be among the residue of people, or to be one of the pure in heart and lay claim to Zion?

We have no physical descriptions of Enoch's City of Holiness—whether it stood on a hill or in a valley, or if it was surrounded by a wall, and so on—but we do know the community was blessed, and "lo, Zion, in process of time, was taken up into heaven. And the Lord said unto Enoch: Behold mine abode forever" (Moses 7:21). What a miraculous group of people, worthy to dwell with God! They achieved this total oneness without brainwashing or genetic alterations. Enoch taught his people to live together in love, and gradually they were endowed with the spiritual characteristics of godliness. What consecration to the Lord! Therefore, "the Lord called his people ZION, because they were of one heart and one mind, and dwelt in righteousness; and there was no poor among them" (v. 18).

Zion's people are of celestial quality, filled with pure love. That's how I want to be. Hope to be. Pray to be.

Conclusion

Life on earth is the "time to prepare to meet God" (Alma 12:24–25). In our eternal quest to become like God the Father and His Son, the Savior set a flawless example of how to develop holy attributes and qualify for exaltation. Perhaps it's not until we figuratively bleed at every pore and fully submit to the Father's will that we can say, as Jesus did, "I have finished the work which thou gavest me to do" (John 17:4).

When, for the moment, we ourselves are not being stretched on a particular cross, we ought to be at the foot of someone else's—full of empathy and proffering spiritual refreshment....

When you and I are unduly impatient, we are suggesting that we like our timetable better than God's. And thus, while the scriptural phrase "in process of time" means "eventually," it also denotes an entire spiritual process: "The Lord showed unto Enoch all the inhabitants of the earth; and he beheld, and lo, Zion, in process of time, was taken up into heaven" (Moses 7:21).

By itself, of course, the passage of time does not bring an automatic advance. Yet, like the prodigal son, we often need the "process of time" in order to come to our spiritual senses (Luke 15:17). [Neal A. Maxwell, "Endure It Well," *Ensign*, May 1990, 34].

How many trials and tests will it take until we attain eternal life? Only our Father knows. Numerous explorers sought after a fountain of youth to provide restorative treatment. However, the fountain God's children need is Christ's living water, which is "a well of water springing up into everlasting life" (John 4:14).

Because of His inestimable love for us, our Father sent His Son to show us the way back to a celestial home. Our goal is to "continue in the faith grounded and settled, and be not moved away from the hope of the gospel" (Colossians 1:23). Each of God's children has the agency to decide what sacrifices we're willing to make to acquire the characteristics of godliness. Remember that with each thought, word, feeling, or act, we are either becoming more like our Savior and our Father, or we are not. There is no middle ground.

The spiritually settled will finally overcome, and the glorious promise is, "To him that overcometh will I grant to sit with me in my throne, even as I also overcame, and am set down with my Father in his throne" (Revelation 3:21).

Meanwhile, let us remember "what manner of persons [we] ought... to be" (2 Peter 3:11; 3 Nephi 27:27). Attributively, we are to become even as Jesus, with His virtues being increasingly replicated in our lives. Even in the midst of our obvious imperfections, a sacred process is to be underway—if slowly, nevertheless resolutely. Whatever one's unfolding agendum, he can be *overcoming* if he is *becoming* more like Christ! [Neal A. Maxwell, "Overcome... Even As I Also Overcame," *Ensign*, May 1987, 72, italics in the original.]

Jesus Christ is the resurrection and the life. Those who become like Him by emulating his virtues will receive resurrection and life eternal, which means to dwell with the Father and Son forever and ever. May this be our ever-present and sacred goal.

For additional insight see:

David A. Bednar, "Tender Mercies of the Lord," *Ensign*, May 2005, 99–102.

Neal A. Maxwell, "The Omniscience of an Omnipotent and Omniloving God," *All These Things Shall Give Thee Experience*, Salt Lake City, Deseret Book Co., 1979, 6–27.

Russell M. Nelson, "Divine Love," *Ensign*, Feb. 2003, 20–25.

Robert D. Hales, "Out of Darkness into His Marvelous Light," *Ensign*, May 2002, 69–72.

And thus they become new creatures;
and unless they do this,
they can in nowise inherit the kingdom of God.
Mosiah 27:26

Inherit the Kingdom of God

The sublime attributes of godliness are of inestimable number. Each is worthy of emulation: mercy, love, goodness, hope, knowledge, meekness, submission, joy, forgiveness, virtue, kindness, faith, compassion, wholeness, holiness, humility, peace, charity, sacrifice, and so on. We've been sent to earth to acquire these characteristics—thus qualifying for advancement in the kingdom of God. "And thus they become new creatures; and unless they do this, they shall in nowise inherit the kingdom of God" (Mosiah 27:26). Our eventual goal is to become gods and goddesses. In other words, we must shed our humanness and take on our true identity. We're not animals, nor fish nor fowl. We aren't Martians or aliens from another planet—though our spirits probably originated from a planet near Kolob. Actually, we're not mere humans, nor are we angels—at least not yet. But Hallelujah! We are of the race of Gods!

As always in spiritual matters, the example and teachings of Jesus are paramount. His oneness with the Father reminds us that our unity with Deity should be a prominent goal—daily, yearly, even hourly. During a dialogue with the Jews, Jesus came nigh to being stoned for saying, "I and my Father are one" (John 10:30).

> Then the Jews took up stones again to stone him.
>
> Jesus answered them, Many good works have I shewed you from Father; for which of those works do ye stone me?
>
> The Jews answered him, saying, For a good work we stone thee not; but for blasphemy; and because that thou, being a man, makest thyself God.
>
> Jesus answered them, Is it not written in your law, I said, Ye are gods?…
>
> If I do not the works of my Father, believe me not.
>
> But if I do, though ye believe not me, believe the works: that ye may know, and believe, that the Father is in me, and I in him (John 10:31–34, 37–38).

From this scene we can first learn that even the ancient Mosaic law offered proof that we are "gods." Secondly, if we truly are sons and daughters of God, it must be exhibited by doing His work. That is how to qualify for the glorious distinction of godhood. "Those who have been born unto God through obedience to the Gospel may by valiant devotion to righteousness obtain exaltation and even reach the status of Godhood." [Joseph F. Smith, "The Father and the Son: A Doctrinal Exposition by the First Presidency and the Twelve," *Improvement Era*, Aug. 1916, 935.]

Valiant devotion to righteousness. What a splendid phrase! That's not something found online via the internet, though many think all knowledge is found within the vast computer highway. However, a course in how to achieve Godhood is not available. Relief Society sisters cannot make quilts online for humanitarian aid, nor can the elders administer to the sick via the internet. Some things still require "hands-on" efforts---without "hands-on" a computer keyboard or mouse. The point is that there is one—uno, primo—only one way to achieve the status of godhood: to emulate Jesus Christ and rely on His merits. Revelations to Joseph Smith clarify the qualities of those who receive celestial exaltation:

Wherefore, as it is written, they are gods, even the sons of God—

Wherefore, all things are theirs, whether life or death, or things present, or things to come, all are theirs and they are Christ's, and Christ is God's.

And they shall overcome all things.

Wherefore, let no man glory in man, but rather let him glory in God,...

These shall dwell in the presence of God and his Christ forever and ever.

These are they whom he shall bring with him, when he shall come in the clouds of heaven to reign on the earth over his people.

These are they who shall have part in the first resurrection....

These are they who shall come forth in the resurrection of the just.

These are they who are come unto Mount Zion, and unto the city of the living God, the heavenly place, the holiest of all....

These are they whose names are written in heaven, where God and Christ are the judge of all.

There are they who are just men made perfect through Jesus the mediator of the new covenant, who wrought out this perfect atonement through the shedding of his own blood (D&C 76:58–59, 62–65, 68–69).

No one can achieve perfection without the mercy and grace of Christ's atonement. It will take each individual's persistent effort, combined with the power of His redemption. President Joseph F. Smith reaffirmed our diligent effort needed to "attain to the glory and exaltation which God designed...."

In other words, we must become like [God]; peradventure to sit upon thrones, to have dominion, power, and eternal increase. God designed this in the beginning. We are the children of God. He is an eternal being, without beginning of days or end of years.… Our tabernacles are to become immortal as his became immortal, that the spirit and the body may be joined together and become one living being, indivisible, inseparable, eternal. [Joseph F. Smith, *Gospel Doctrine*, 62-64.]

Prize the Good

None of us are as perfect as Jesus, so we must undergo tests which teach us to prize the good, rather than the evil. This starts at birth and continues until we rest beneath gravestones—well, on second thought, it may go on indefinitely in eternity, because we can't instantly become gods and goddesses. Every day on earth, we confront decisions of eternal significance, though we may not recognize them as such. Even in childhood, when choices are small and superficial, we must learn to select correct choices.

One day as a child of six, I literally picked the wrong choice. My father had built our first home with a large backyard that included a garden and orchard. While playing outside with my siblings or friends, we often nibbled on fresh peas in pods or pulled up carrots to wash in the hose, then crunch and munch. I remember how the fruit trees yielded peaches, apricots, and plums so fresh that juice ran down our chins and splotched our clothes. Of course, Mom always noticed the stains while doing the laundry, yet she never scolded us about eating the freshly-picked produce, because that was healthy snacking—though it meant fewer bottles to preserve for our year's supply. The only complaint I once overheard was when Mom said to Dad that we never harvested as many cherries as she hoped. It seemed that the birds always got them first.

One fine summer afternoon, my friend Mary had come to play in our yard, and, lucky for us, my siblings weren't around to bother us. We had a new baby brother in our house, and my older sister and younger brother were probably paying attention to him. Being a rambunctious child, I knew it was rare for someone not to be watching my actions and antics.

After using considerable energy on the backyard swing set, I motioned Mary to follow me to the garden and orchard, where I hoped to find something to snack on. That's when I saw the cherry tree with acorn-sized fruit, but still quite green. I remembered Mom's comment that birds took most of the cherries before we could eat them.

I raced to the cherry tree and swung up into the V of the branches. It was a dwarf tree, easily climbable by a six-year-old tomboy. Mary, who wasn't as daring as I, simply watched while I braced myself among the limbs and snatched two green cherries. Popping them in my mouth, I chewed carefully, then spit the pits on the ground. Then I grabbed two more cherries and dropped them into Mary's palm. She didn't hesitate any more than I had to chomp into them. I saw no adverse signs on her face that the fruit was sour or otherwise unpalatable. Eagerly, I reached for several more clumps of cherries, which I dropped for Mary to catch in her skirt, which she held out like a shallow bowl.

It didn't take long before I'd gathered all the cherries I could reach, and Mary's skirt was rather loaded down. Perhaps it was good that the cherries were still green; otherwise, her dress might have been stained with red spots. Carefully, we maneuvered toward the back of the lot, where the two of us sat on the steps that led down to the mid-block alley. One by one, and sometimes two by two, we gobbled up our harvest of green cherries. There couldn't have been more than fifty or sixty that we ate, but I don't remember any revulsion while chewing and swallowing them. When we finished, a scatter of small pits lay around us, and we brushed the few remaining stems and leaves off Mary's dress. Then we happily walked toward my house to report what we'd done.

I can still vividly see the moment. Mom sat ironing in the laundry room. I didn't see the baby, so I assumed he was napping. From the living room came the sound of a children's show on the television, which likely had captivated my sister and brother. We'd only had the television for a year—still a rare luxury in 1956—but if it was a choice to watch TV or go outside, I always choose the latter. In fact, I still rarely sit down in front of a television—far too sedate for my active lifestyle.

Anyway, when I found Mom seated at the ironing board, I touched her shoulder and said with enthusiasm, "Guess what, Mom? You don't have to worry about the birds getting the cherries this year. Me and Mary ate 'em all."

"What?" Mom set the iron down, then turned to look directly at me. Sitting on a chair, she was eye-to-eye with me.

"Me and Mary ate the cherries. They were green, but they tasted pretty good. Now the birds won't get them."

Mary remained silent, so Mom turned toward her. My friend nodded to affirm what we'd done. Was it my imagination, or was her face a little green at that moment?

Shoving her chair back from the ironing board, Mom abruptly stood and walked through the kitchen to reach the phone. Three calls were made in quick succession: to our pediatrician, to Mary's mother, and to my father at work. The doctor said our escapade didn't sound too serious, though green cherries would likely give little girls tummy aches. Mary's mother said to send her daughter home immediately. My father only chuckled. Mom hung up the phone, then sadly shook her head at Mary and me.

As happens after making poor decisions, I had to endure the consequences: my friend was sent home, and I was sentenced to stay inside—true punishment for an outdoorsy gal like me. Luckily, by the time Dad came home from work, I'd had no stomach upsets from eating the green cherries. But that's not always the case, when wrong choices are made—especially where eternal principles are involved. Most decisions result in either a reward or consequence—depending on whether we choose good or evil. Each time we select righteousness, the Lord blesses us with greater faith and enhanced courage to become what we were created to be: gods and goddesses.

Becoming Gods and Goddesses

Modern-day revelation provides tremendous insight about becoming gods and goddesses, such as this eloquent message from President John Taylor:

What is [man]? He had his being in the eternal worlds; he existed before he came here. He is not only the Son of man, but he is the Son of God also. He is a God in embryo, and possesses within him a spark of that eternal flame which was struck from the blaze of God's eternal fire in the eternal world, and is placed here upon the earth that he may possess true intelligence, true light, true knowledge—that he may know himself—that he may know God—that he may know something about what he was before he came here—that he may know something about what he is destined to enjoy in the eternal worlds… that he may understand his true relationship to God.…

What is man? A god, even the son [or daughter] of God, possessing noble aspirations, holy feelings, that may be governed by virtuous principles, possessing elevated ideas,…

This is what man is, if he lives the religion of heaven, and performs faithfully those things God has appointed him to do, that he may increase from intelligence to intelligence, and go on with that eternal progression, not only in this world, but in worlds without end. [John Taylor, remarks made in the Tabernacle, Great Salt Lake City, February 19, 1860.]

There is no indication that godhood is an easy goal to achieve— though the rewards for doing so are immense and everlasting. There's no way to pretend to be something we're not. We cannot simply don a costume, like a child on Halloween, to become a knight in shining armor or a princess with a gleaming tiara. However, the hope is that we will prove ourselves worthy to receive a crown of glory as kings and queens in the kingdom of God.

Crown of Glory

Through life on earth we learn that spiritual achievements require diligence, dedication, and perseverance. Each must "work out your own salvation with fear and trembling before him" (Mormon 9:27). Our Father knows we will better appreciate the hereafter if we've struggled and sacrificed to achieve celestial rewards. When we prove ourselves worthy, we'll be "crowned with honor, and glory, and immortality, and eternal life" (D&C 75:5).

Prophetic revelation keeps Latter-day Saints focused on heavenly goals. "But as it is written, Eye hath not seen, nor ear heard, neither have entered into the heart of man, the things which God hath prepared for them that love him" (1 Corinthians 2:9). Though a veil has been drawn over our memories of pre-earthly life, we did have foreknowledge of the celestial rewards awaiting us. "Wherefore the day cometh when ye shall be crowned with much glory" (D&C 58:3–4).

It's doubtful we'll receive an actual crown of glory like what kids get at Burger King for their birthdays. A better image is an angel's halo, though there's no mention of halos in scripture. Perhaps a crown of light is the best image to represent the spiritual reward of earning the celestial kingdom.

> You are heirs to great fortunes, for eternal life is the greatest gift.
>
> What will you do with it? You are entitled to a kingdom or a queendom. You are princesses and princes. Do you prize your inheritance?
>
> The king's highway—the royal road to eternal joys and exaltation—is a hard road, full of sacrifices and restriction and hard work. The way is narrow, but it is straight, well-marked, and strongly-beamed....
>
> The permanent kingdom is yours, not for the asking, but for the earning.
>
> Will you abdicate it? That is much easier than to claim it. Will you... voluntarily renounce the throne? And through carelessness and heedlessness voluntarily relinquish your right to this powerful and blessed privilege? Will you forfeit your crown? [Spencer W. Kimball, "Kings and Priests" *BYU Speeches of the Year*, 15 Feb. 1966, 17–18.]

Christ "shall deliver up the kingdom, and present it unto the Father, spotless,... then shall he be crowned with the crown of his glory, to sit on the throne of his power to reign forever and ever (D&C 76:107–108). We are to "be a crown of glory in the hand of the Lord, and a royal diadem in the hand of God" (Isaiah 62:3).

Wow! A royal diadem in the hand of God! Forget about being "all that you can be in the Army." Never mind seeking for sunken pirate treasure. There is no greater goal you and I can obtain than to be an heir of God.

> They shall be heirs of God and joint heirs with Jesus Christ. What is it? To inherit the same power, the same glory and the same exaltation, until you arrive at the station of a god, and ascend the throne of eternal power, the same as those who have gone before. What did Jesus do? Why I do the things I saw my Father do when worlds came rolling into existence. My Father worked out His kingdom with fear and trembling, and I must do the same; and when I get my kingdom I shall present it to My Father, so that He may obtain kingdom upon kingdom, and it will exalt Him in His glory. He will then take a higher exaltation, and I will take His place, and thereby become exalted myself. So that Jesus treads in the tracks of His Father, and inherits what God did before; and God is thus glorified and exalted in the salvation and exaltation of all His children....
>
> It will be a great while after you have passed through the veil before you have learned [the principles of exaltation]. It is not all to be comprehended in this world; it will be a great work to learn our salvation and exaltation even beyond the grave. [Joseph Smith, *History of the Church*, 6:306–307.]

Our crowns of righteousness will not diminish God's glory in any way; but rather, our exaltation will render added honor and majesty to both the Father and Son.

Celestial Homesickness

Because our physical constitutions are imperfect and subject to frailties, diseases, and decay, most of us are eager for the renewal of our bodies at the time of resurrection. Though composed of earthly elements, we must remember to think and act according to the spark of divinity within us. Indeed "there is within each of us a giant struggling with celestial homesickness" (Howard W. Hunter, "What Is Greatness?" *Ensign*, Sept. 1987, 70).

In recent decades, medical science has improved and given hope of healing to many with formerly untreatable diseases. However,, no one wants to hear a doctor say "cancer." But gratefully, many of today's treatments can cause tumors to go into remission and sometimes fully eradicate them. My father-in-law owned a sheep ranch, where he also grew alfalfa and barley for feed. Farming meant long hours of sun exposure—at a time before ultraviolet rays were known to be harmful. Now he makes regular visits to a dermatologist, who diagnoses and burns away skin cancers on his face and arms.

Though we dread physical diseases that weaken the body's immune system, such as skin cancer, a higher concern is *sin cancer*—a disease that weakens our spirits. Like cancer cells that overtake normal tissues in the body, sin can overcome our spirits if we don't get proper treatment. When we kneel in prayer with real intent before our Father, He can carefully diagnose and burn away any impurities. It won't be painless nor tearless. Those with sin cancer will endure intense grief, guilt, remorse, and repentance before becoming worthy of celestial life with God. Yet each treatment is crucial in the process of purification.

When the frailties and imperfections of immortality are left behind, in the glorified state of the blessed hereafter, husband and wife will administer in their respective stations, [seeing] and understanding alike and co-operating to the full in the government of their family kingdom. Then shall woman be recompensed in rich measure for all the injustice that womanhood has endured in mortality. Then shall woman reign by Divine right, a queen in the resplendent realm of her glorified state, even as exalted man shall stand, priest and king unto the Most High God. (James E. Talmage, *Young Women's Journal*, October 1914, 602–603).

Walk in Newness of Life

My own appreciation for life grew tenfold while spending a month in the hospital during 2005. Funny thing, I had just turned fifty-five—the age at which the AARP seriously recruits new members. In a sense, this major health crisis was my initiation to old age. The last day of January, I underwent routine surgery: a bladder lift, which is common for women in their late fifties. I expected immediate and permanent recovery. But not so. Complications set in. I was not released for thirty-one days. Then I was homebound for several more months trying to regain my health and vigor. What a hopeless time it was, yet what a learning experience!

The strange part is that I keep my body in good physical condition. Nearly every day, I exercise in our fitness room, swim, hike, ski, or walk four miles. My condominium neighbors, many over the age of eighty, were aware of my desire to stay fit. When they found out how sick I was, they said to my husband, "If Bonnie's in the hospital, then the rest of us are really in trouble."

Doctors are still unsure why my healthy body reacted the way it did. The surgical procedure went very well, but when I was allowed to eat again, my gastrointestinal tract shut down. I began vomiting. My intestines stopped working, and my abdomen became distended with pain. X-rays showed that my bowels were swollen with inflammation. The small intestines were triple their normal width: three to four inches in diameter, rather than one.

A nurse put a flexible tube down my nose into my stomach to drain out fluid, which the stomach produces constantly. My abdomen was so distended that I appeared to be pregnant with triplets. Pain was intense and constant. Waves of nausea became my worst enemy. I was not allowed to eat or drink, though occasionally I could suck ice chips to ease mouth dryness. An intravenous drip of saline solution kept my body hydrated by going directly into my veins, thus circumventing the digestive tract. I was also put on oxygen to improve my blood gases. Many days I was wheeled to radiology for x-rays to see what more could be done. But nothing changed. My bowels simply refused to perform their proper functions.

When normal intestinal peristalsis shuts down, the medical term is ileus, or in my case postoperative paralytic ileus. This life-threatening condition is usually caused by an intestinal blockage, though it can be triggered by surgery, anesthetics, head injury, sepsis, trauma to the spine, or other medical conditions.

Ten agonizing days passed with no improvement. My situation seemed hopeless. One nurse said it was good I had brown hair; without that they would never see me, since my face was so white that it blended right into the sheets. A general surgeon suggested exploratory surgery to look for intestinal blockages. So once again I was wheeled to the operating room.

The surgeon found no obstructions in the endless tubular rows of swollen intestines. However, he did all he could in hopes of improving peristalsis. After I'd awakened from surgery, he explained the procedure. When inflammation occurs, the tissues get sticky, resulting in adhesions. This means that instead of lying in smooth and evenly laid out tubes, my distended bowels were stuck together in clumps. After thoroughly checking the to make sure there were no obstructions, the surgeon replaced my bowels in nice even rows and put a mesh material between them to prevent more adhesions. He also removed my appendix, which was stuck within a clump of intestines. Though undergoing a second surgery could aggravate my already dreary situation, it was the best any doctor could do. Now I would simply have to play the waiting game to see if my intestines would awaken and start to work on their own.

Because I'd already been without food for ten days, a pair of nurses came to put an intravenous feeding line into my upper left arm. A special liquid formula was prepared for me daily—of course, hospitals aren't known for their gourmet meals—but I didn't have to eat it. Rather, the wholesome fluid pumped into the tube in my upper arm vein, then directly to my heart, where the pure nourishment could circulate through my bloodstream.

A series of wonderful nurses watched over me and tried to keep me comfortable with anti-nausea shots and pain medication. My doctors came daily to consult with me and give me hope. Every afternoon, my husband, Glenn, left work early to be with me, and he stayed until eight or nine, when I would send him home. Like most men, he wanted to fix or repair the problem. But Glenn felt helpless to do anything, and his presence at my bedside was actually more draining than uplifting for either of us.

My mother visited several times, bringing flowers and encouraging words, and my youngest son and his wife came to cheer me up, as did a few of my closest friends. Our children and grandchildren, who lived out of town, phoned, e-mailed, and sent get-well cards. But week after week, I remained unhealed and miserable. When my bishop and his wife stopped by, he asked if I would welcome visits from members of our ward or stake. With the graveness of my condition, I said, "No. I just need to rest."

During any prolonged hospital stay or bed rest, pneumonia is always a threat. This was especially critical for me, since my abdomen was so vastly distended that I could not fully inflate my lungs. Thus, whenever I spiked a fever, someone would whisk me downstairs for x-rays to see if my lungs had filled with fluid. Thankfully, they remained clear.

Everyone who cared for me said I was an extreme case. Rarely does a patient have a stomach tube for more than one week—and some who can't stand it pull it out prematurely, then deal with the nausea in another way. My stomach tube remained in place four weeks! What a horrible, terrible ordeal! My bowels continued to be silent and dysfunctional, and my belly remained distended and painful. There were times I would just lie in my bed and moan and cry, especially while alone at night.

Despite the pain, isolation, and nausea, the most profound anguish I faced came on Sundays. In the LDS Hospital is a branch of the LDS Church that meets each Sunday morning. I was too sick to attend my first week in the hospital, but thereafter, with all my tubes and treatments, I would be taken in a wheelchair down the elevator to sacrament meeting. My first time there, "Oh, My Father" (*Hymns*, #292) was the opening hymn. "O my Father, thou that dwellest/ In the high and glorious place,/ When shall I regain thy presence/ And again behold thy face?" Though I didn't have the energy to sing, I pondered every line. In my frail health, I wondered if my destiny was to "leave this frail existence, [and] lay this body by; Father, Mother, may I greet you, in your royal courts on high?" As shiver raced down my spine as both joy and anxiety washed over me. What a sublime moment it would be to arrive at such a state of grace! How I yearned to see my Heavenly Father and Mother, as well as my Savior Jesus Christ.

Tears pooled in my eyes. I wasn't ready to die! I had a zest for life and for people, and I didn't want to leave my loved ones behind. As the hymn continued, I sent a silent prayer upward, asking, "Father have I 'completed all you sent me forth to do'? Have I truly done everything I can to make myself worthy to 'come and dwell with you'?"

A serene feeling warmed my soul. I felt my Heavenly Parents were nearby. And I knew that through the grace of Christ's Atonement, I could rise again. Whether I died as a result of this present illness or recovered and my demise came at a later date, the crucial matter was that I endure to the end with faith, hope, and charity. As long as I lived, I would know that the divine Father, Mother, and Son were only a prayer away, especially in the hospital's dreary, lonely nights.

On that Sabbath day at the hospital, another profound lesson touched my soul. More poignant than the thought-provoking hymn was the moment when priesthood brethren passed the sacrament. Since my medical condition didn't allow me to eat or drink, I couldn't partake of the bread and water. Though I longed to renew the sacred covenants I'd made, it was impossible. For the next few weeks, tears wet my cheeks each Sunday when I had to pass aside the sacramental trays that were provided in remembrance of Christ's body and blood. How I yearned to let Him know of my gratitude for His infinite and merciful Atonement!

Though I couldn't partake of the emblems, I could covenant to always remember Him.

I knew Jesus had suffered not only for the sins of all mankind, including my own, but also He had sacrificed His life for "the pains and the sicknesses of his people" (Alma 7:11). That struck me as significant during each day I lay sick and pain-filled in my solitary hospital room. The more anguish I felt, the more I could identify with the agony Christ suffered.

During my illness, I often prayed that Heavenly Father would take away the bitter pain which I could barely tolerate. I humbled myself, I wept, I trembled, and I begged to be blessed and healed. Often, I recalled the agony Christ suffered as He bled from every pore during His prayer in Gethsemane. Though I earnestly appealed to have my bitter cup removed, never once did I have the courage to say, "Father, not my will, but thine be done." I wanted to be cured. I wanted not to leave this frail existence, but to leave the hospital—and not in a hearse. I begged for release from my suffering, but I could not make myself say "Thy will be done." Not even in a small degree could I submit to our Father in the same manner as the Savior did.

Though Jesus had felt the torment of the entire world's iniquity upon Him, and I just had abdominal pain, I could not bear it nobly and bravely as Christ had done. I was unable to put "off the natural man, and [become] a saint through the Atonement of Christ," and be "meek, humble, patient, full of love, [and] willing to submit to all that the Father seeth to inflict" (Mosiah 3:19).

Perhaps that's why my illness was prolonged—so I could learn to be more humble and submissive before my Heavenly Father. I am in total awe that Jesus had the power to lay aside His own desires and fully submit to the Father's will. What a long stretch I must make in striving to become like Him. How hard I must work to become pure, sanctified, and worthy someday to dwell in His presence.

One day after giving me a blessing, my bishop suggested that our ward members fast and pray for me on the upcoming Sunday. I agreed it was a good idea. And hallelujah! By the next Tuesday, my nausea subsided, and I was able to drink a little juice. The next day I progressed to chicken broth and green Jell-o, part of a Utahn's staple diet. Soon I was released and came home to spend a slow six months recovering my strength. By autumn, I felt blessed to "walk in newness of life" (Romans 6:4). Though my body had grown weaker in the hospital, my spirit was strengthened by more clearly understanding the role of the Savior's atoning sacrifice.

Bodily renewal is an ample blessing, but becoming a new creature spiritually is far superior. Without the atonement of Jesus Christ it's inconceivable, impossible—our progress toward eternal life is stonewalled. We remain in iniquity and darkness. Unclean. Unredeemed.

> I suggest that in our fallen state we are like buckets filled with filthy water. Our Savior comes along, sees our plight, and if we choose to ask him to help us, he dumps out the water. He then turns to the laborious task of cleansing the bucket. He grinds, and he scrubs, and he scours. It hurts abominably. Nevertheless, when the process of cleansing is complete, the bucket is something to behold—it shines. But the cleanup is not yet complete, for the bucket does not fulfill its rightful role until we have invited the Savior to fill it, this time with living water....
>
> This great exchange manifests itself in what we know as the "mighty change" (Mosiah 5:2). It is mighty in the sense that it is God-inspired, God-directed, and God-empowered. This change is neither superficial nor cosmetic. It does not result in skin-deep holiness. It is not just the result of self-control or willpower. It is a change born of the Spirit and empowered by him who delights in remaking the human heart.... In a word, the values of a person who is a new creature in Christ undergoes a transformation. It is a mighty change. [Robert L. Millet, *Alive in Christ: The Miracle of Spiritual Rebirth*, 50–51.]

How magnificent, how glorious, how astounding! Our lives can be renewed through Christ! What must we do to achieve this blessing? First, our hearts must be broken and our spirits contrite. Then we must exercise extraordinary faith, maintain an eagerness to change, and keep our eyes forever focused on the Lord.

An Eye Single to the Glory of God

Because Jesus Christ was the only sinless man to walk the earth, only He could demonstrate the way to obtain eternal life. There is but one set of footprints that mark the strait and narrow path home to our Father. Jesus constantly beckons to us during our earthly sojourn that we might follow Him and be saved— physically and spiritually, as illustrated in the following verses:

> And as Jesus passed by, he saw a man which was blind from his birth,…
>
> [Jesus said] As long as I am in the world, I am the light of the world.
>
> When he had thus spoken, he spat on the ground, and made clay of the spittle, and he anointed the eyes of the blind man with the clay.
>
> And said unto him, Go, wash in the pool of Siloam, (which is by interpretation, Sent). He went his way therefore, and washed and came seeing (John 9:1, 5–7).

The symbolism in this miracle is stunning. Jesus made clay and anointed the eyes of the blind man that he might see. In a similar manner, because Christ is the Light of the World, He can symbolically anoint our eyes to allow us new vision through spiritual lenses. Though our earthly sojourn may be fraught with clutter and confusion, after we wash away the clay and spittle of this world, we can more clearly behold the things of eternity. This divine perspective will always remain with us, if we live worthy to have the constant companionship of the Holy Ghost, and thus, bask in the Light of Christ.

During the meridian of time, Jesus taught His disciples, "The light of the body is the eye: if therefore thine eye be single [to the glory of God], thy whole body shall be full of light" (Matthew

6:22). An eye single to the glory of God has nothing to do with winking and squinting nor putting a patch over one eye, although Christ did say, "if thy eye offend thee, pluck it out: it is better for thee to enter into the kingdom of God with one eye, than having two eyes to be cast into hell fire" (Mark 9:47). Rather, we are to keep both our eyes focused on the glory of God.

In the latter-days, the Lord revealed to Joseph Smith, "And if your eye be single to my glory, your whole bodies shall be filled with light, and there shall be no darkness in you; and that body which is filled with light comprehendeth all things" (D&C 88:67). There are few blessings better than ridding ourselves of darkness in order to be filled with godly light. Imagine being able to comprehend all things!

> Nevertheless, the day shall come when you shall comprehend even God, being quickened in him and by him.
>
> Then shall ye know that ye have seen me, that I am and that I am the true light that is in you, and that you are in me; otherwise you could not abound (D&C 88:49–50).

Without Jesus Christ, you and I cannot abound in this life or the next. Neither can there be peace on the earth and in the souls of God's children without the True Light illuminating their souls. For Jesus came "that they might have life, and that they might have it abundantly" (John 10:10). So I must ask myself how I can better become a beacon for Christ and hold up His "light that it may shine unto the world" (3 Nephi 18:24). What must I do to follow the Lord's resounding words, "Let your light so shine before men, that they may see your good works, and glorify your Father which is in heaven" (Matthew 5:16).

How grateful we are to know our Savior will light the pathway home so we might, in turn, light the way for others! As in the fairy tale of Hansel and Gretel, Jesus has left us a trail of bread crumbs to follow—sacred, sacramental bread, as a token of His Atonement. The strait and narrow path will also be splotched with His holy blood and tears, which He shed for our salvation.

Not only has Jesus provided a perfect example for us to follow, but also a perfect atonement and resurrection to free the world from sin and pain. Never forget Christ's promise, "Behold, I am the light and the life of the world; and... I have glorified the Father in taking upon me the sins of the world, in the which I have suffered the will of the Father in all things from the beginning" (3 Nephi 11:11).

Conclusion

We rejoice in Jesus Christ, who "proceedeth forth from the presence of God to fill the immensity of space—The light which is in all things, which giveth life to all things, which is the law by which all things are governed" (D&C 88:12–13).

What a marvelous work and a wonder when men and women come unto Christ and, through His merits, become new creatures! Jesus is not merely a scientist, as were the fictional men who created the new creatures we know as Frankenstein and Edward Scissorhands. He is the Beloved Son of God, our Savior and Redeemer, who can create celestial beings out of mere mortals. "Therefore if any man be in Christ, he is a new creature: old things are passed away; behold, all things are become new" (2 Corinthians 5:17).

Each small miracle that hones our hearts and souls will gradually carve us into the celestial form our Father intended us to receive. "Wherefore, be not weary in well-doing, for ye are laying the foundation of a great work. And out of small things proceedeth that which is great" (D&C 64:33). God's great work is to transform our imperfect beings into gods or goddesses. It's each individual's choice whether or not we allow this miracle of advancement to occur.

Mankind are organized of element designed to endure all eternity; [we] never had a beginning and never can have an end... [We are] brought together, organized, and capacitated to receive knowledge and intelligence, to be enthroned in glory, to be made angels, Gods—beings who will hold control over the elements, and have power by their word to command the creation and redemption of the world, or to extinguish suns by their breath, and disorganize worlds, hurling them back into their chaotic state. This is what you and I are created for. [Brigham Young, *Journal of Discourses*, 3:356.]

For additional insight see:

Truman G. Madsen, *The Radiant Life*, Salt Lake City, Bookcraft, 1994.

Jeffrey R. Holland, "The Grandeur of God," *Ensign*, November, 2003,70–73.

Therefore, what manner of men ought ye to be?
Verily I say unto you, even as I am.
3 Nephi 27:27

More, Savior, Like Thee

Become even as Jesus Christ. Can that be possible? The Savior is the most triumphant hero we revere. However, He is not known to be faster than a speeding bullet nor more powerful than a locomotive, as was Superman; nor can He throw sticky webs like Spiderman to suspend himself from any surface. The problem with such super heroes is that they are fictitious, while Jesus is real, and He truly can save the world in a super, supernal way. Someday, the heavens will explode with signs and wonders, and we will gaze heavenward to say, "Look, it's a bird! It's a plane! No, it's Jesus Christ! He is coming to reign on earth for a thousand years!"

Prophesies state that rainbows will cease to appear during the year of Christ's advent. Though I can't imagine not gazing in wonder at those brilliant arcs of color in the sky, it's more difficult to conceive of the multitude of heavenly events which will cause the entire world to be awestruck at the Lord's Second Coming.

An angel "shall sound his trump both long and loud, and all nations shall hear it" (D&C 88:94). We will hardly believe our eyes and ears when "the Lord himself shall descend from heaven with a shout, with the voice of the archangel, and with the trump of

God, and the dead in Christ shall rise first" (Thessalonians 4:16). How stunning the skies will be when "the face of the Lord shall be unveiled" (D&C 88:95)! Then the righteous and worthy saints "that are upon the earth, who are alive, shall be quickened and shall be caught up to meet him" (v. 96). Those who have become like Christ with "a mighty change wrought in their hearts" by receiving "his image in [their] countenances" (Alma 5:13–14), will qualify to "ever be with the Lord" (Thessalonians 4:17). There is no greater blessing than to live with God forever.

The challenge to be worthy of everlasting life is not meant to discourage us. Rather, it is a privilege to learn to emulate Christ. Many rewards await us. Through the grace of His Atonement, we can partake of tremendous love and happiness—in this life as well as the next. That's what occurred in the Promised Land after Jesus visited Lehi's descendants. His presence and teachings had such a lasting impact that for two hundred years there was "no contention in the land, because of the love of God which did dwell in the hearts of the people,... and surely there could not be a happier people among all the people who had been created by the hand of God" (4 Nephi 1:15–16). These humble people not only listened to Christ's words, but they also applied His gospel in their personal lives—thus acquiring more joy, love, and peace to live in harmony. They stretched their souls and arose to His admonition, "Therefore, what manner of men ought ye to be? Verily I say unto you, even as I am" (3 Nephi 27:27). That counsel remains in effect for all of God's children—today and forever. What a holy and ambitious challenge for each of us!

"The more we know of Jesus, the more we will love Him. The more we know of Jesus, the more we will trust Him. The more we know of Jesus, the more we will want to be like Him and to be with Him by becoming the manner of men and women that He wishes us to be" (Neal A. Maxwell, "Plow in Hope," Conference Report, Apr. 2001, 59). This quote's significance is heightened because Elder Maxwell said it while undergoing intense treatment for leukemia. No doubt his lengthy trial of sickness and pain gave him unique understanding of Jesus' anguish at Gethsemane and Golgotha.

Taste the Bitter

Do you remember the time before vaccines could prevent children from suffering many diseases? When our oldest son attended third grade, chicken pox spread throughout his classroom and rendered half the children absent for a week. Our son, in turn, shared chicken pox with his three siblings in quick succession. Our middle son and daughter became more feverish, sick, and itchy than their older brother had been. However, the baby, who was eighteen months, broke out with only four pox on his torso and never became too fussy. This is parallel to our sojourn on earth. Some children of God require light cases of temptation and trials to immunize them against the cares of the world and prepare them for exaltation. Others are fraught with mighty tests that burn their souls with fever and discomfort. Because our Father knows us individually, He allows adversity to affect our lives in personal ways suited for our spiritual maturation. Thus, one by one, we each must pass through earthly tests which qualify us for the celestial kingdom.

In Christ's quest to bring salvation to all our Father's children, He willingly "drank out of the bitter cup" and "suffered the will of the Father in all things" (3 Nephi 11:11). For us to assist in building the kingdom of God, we, too, must "taste the bitter that [we] may know to prize the good" (Moses 6:55). Please note, however, that we are only required to *taste* the bitter, not gulp down the entire cup like Jesus, who was "led, crucified, and slain,… the will of the Son being swallowed up in the will of the Father (Mosiah 15:7)." Though God the Father desires that we conform our will to His, the bitter cups we're proffered are often made of paper—flimsy and easy to crush if we rely on the atoning blood of Christ. When we remember His sublime example, we can overcome the abrasiveness of life without becoming bitterly sorry for ourselves.

As children of God and spiritual siblings to Jesus, we possess the power to become celestial beings. The hymn, "More Holiness Give Me," gently reminds us to become like our Savior, Jesus Christ.

More holiness give me, More strivings within,
More patience in suff'ring, More sorrow for sin,
More faith in my Savior, More sense of his care,
More joy in his service, More purpose in prayer....
More fit for the kingdom, More used would I be.
More blessed and holy—More, Savior, like thee.
["More Holiness Give Me," *Hymns*, 131.]

Pattern our Lives after Christ

Jesus showed us the pattern, for He was tested in direct proportion to the truth, light, and knowledge He possessed. Therefore, He taught, "For unto whomsoever much is given, of him shall be much required" (Luke 12:48). That means each of us will be tested according to what we're prepared to tolerate and withstand.

We may not live fairy tale lives, in which fairy godmothers wave magic wands or knights in shining armor come to save the day. However, our lives can end "happily ever after," if we are intimately connected to the Father and the Son. Their omniscience and power are available to sustain us through all the upheavals of life—spiritual, mental, emotional, or physical. Because Satan's fiery darts are aimed at us daily, we must steadily hold up our shield of faith. This fast-paced, technological world hurls new temptations at us so fast that we can easily get caught off-guard. That's when I ponder what it might have been like to live in simpler days without computers, jet airplanes, cell phones, guns, recreational vehicles, and jammed highways. Sometimes I wonder if road rage initially began with chariot drivers, like in the movie "Ben Hur."

It's important to emulate the meek and lowly life of Christ. Compared to the worldliness that currently tugs at us like an undertow, the Savior's existence provides quite a humble contrast.

Jesus did not begin to preach His gospel until He reached the age of thirty. By the age of thirty-three, His life ended. Three years was all the time He had, and yet, He became the most influential man in history. But how did He do it? How, in just three years' time, did He become so great?

Jesus was born within a lowly stable in Bethlehem—not in a fancy hospital surrounded by medical personnel and state-of-the-art machinery. Though the royal lineage of David flowed in this baby's blood, His mother Mary did not live like a queen. She was raised in a provincial town as a peasant. Jesus did not sleep in a finely-carved cradle or colorfully decorated crib, but in a rough-hewn manger filled with hay for the stable animals. Shortly after His birth, Mary and her husband Joseph welcomed humble shepherds who came to worship the newborn. Later, visits came from ornamented wise men, bearing precious gifts. Rather than benefitting the child, these honorable events actually threatened His life. To prevent His slaughter by Herod's soldiers, Mary and Joseph fled with the baby to Egypt until it was safe to return to Palestine.

Then this young family settled in the village of Nazareth, where Jesus grew up working alongside Joseph, who was a carpenter. As Jewish custom required, Jesus was schooled in the law and scriptures alongside other boys in the local synagogue. We have no record that He played basketball, soccer, or other boyhood games, nor that He felt a need to dress and act like His peers so they would accept Him.

The unique characteristics of His divine nature made Jesus diverse as "he increased in wisdom and stature, and in favour with God and man" (Luke 2:52). Undoubtedly, Jesus often communed with His Heavenly Father, who taught Him truths that no one on earth could comprehend. However, that did not win Him a scholarship to attend a prestigious college or university. He never earned a master's degree in psychology, nor a doctorate in theology, yet "all that heard him were astonished at his understanding and answers" (Luke 2:47).

Jesus did not own an ornate home nor stay in luxurious hotels when He traveled. Once in a lowly manner, He said, "The foxes have holes and the birds of the air have nests, but the Son of Man hath not where to lay his head" (Matthew 8:20). Scriptures record that He sometimes slept in fishermen's boats—even in the midst of stormy waters. He never bought a view lot overlooking the city of Jerusalem and built a mansion there. Yet He taught that in His Father's house are many mansions, where He will prepare a place for the faithful to dwell.

What Jesus ate was not from fast food drive-up windows, nor was it prepared by skilled chefs in exclusive restaurants. Occasionally, He was invited to dine in people's homes; but more often, He partook of grains or figs, plucked along the wayside while walking from town to town. He never invited multitudes to a massive dining hall to feast upon gourmet delicacies. But on a hillside, Jesus did miraculously feed thousands of people with a few loaves and fishes. He was also known for changing water into wine.

Not prone to wealth, Jesus didn't have a wallet full of credit cards to purchase items of luxury like diamonds and houseboats. He never bargain hunted at advertised sales, warehouse stores, nor factory outlet malls. Content with a simple lifestyle, He did not own a marvelous wardrobe of the latest designer fashions. He had but one coat, which soldiers gambled for at His death. His only pair of sandals were removed when soldiers nailed His feet upon the cross.

So why did people revere Him and esteem His greatness? He never rose to any public office. He didn't become a famous Roman leader like Caesar, nor was He elected as governor or senator. Jesus wasn't called to head a bishopric or high priests group, yet He became the most outstanding High Priest who ever lived, "for he taught them as one having authority" (Matthew 7:29).

Although He never attended medical school, Jesus was known to miraculously cure many faith-filled individuals. With kind words and the gentle touch of His hands, He healed the leprous and the lame, He opened the ears of the deaf, and gave sight to the blind. People also acknowledged that "with authority commandeth he even the unclean spirits and they do obey him" (Mark 1:27). This divine Son of God could calm the perilous sea with the simple words, "Peace be still" (Mark 4:39). He also calmed souls in peril by offering salvation unto those who believed on His words. No wonder He was worshiped and hailed as "King of kings and Lord of lords" (1 Timothy 6:15).

Jesus did nothing to become famous like those we revere in this modern age. He wasn't a sports hero or Olympic athlete. He did not get invited for an interview with Oprah Winfrey or Larry King. He never sang on the radio, never starred in a movie, never wrote a book. Yet hundreds of songs, movies, and books have been written about Jesus. John ends his gospel account in this manner: "And there are also many other things which Jesus did, the which, if they should be written every one, I suppose that even the world itself could not contain the books that should be written. Amen" (John 21:25).

Today, Jesus Christ and His gospel are known worldwide. That's incredible, since His only preaching was in a radius less than 200 miles from where He was born. He never drove a fancy convertible, rode on a high-speed train, flew in a jet, nor blasted off in a space shuttle. His main means of travel was in fishermen's boats, traversing the Sea of Galilee. More often, He went on foot—His sandaled feet getting dusty and dirty along the way.

We have no record of Jesus riding in a glorious horse-drawn chariot as did rulers of His day. However many witnessed Him riding a donkey on His triumphal entry into Jerusalem just a few days before He died. At the gates of the city, people laid clothing and palm branches in His route and hailed Him, "Saying, Blessed be the King that cometh in the name of the Lord: peace in heaven, and glory in the highest." Yet "some of the Pharisees from among the multitude said unto him, Master, rebuke thy disciples." Then Jesus turned "and said unto them, I tell you that, if these should hold their peace, the stones would immediately cry out" (see Luke 19:38–40).

So much divinity in Christ that even the stones longed to shout "Hosanna" to His Holy Name! Indeed, a few days later, the stones did speak forth; however, not in a shout of joy, but in a cry of anguish as the creator of the world was crucified. "Behold, the veil of the temple was rent in twain from the top to the bottom; and the earth did quake, & the rocks rent" (Matthew 27:51). Standing nearby, a centurion, though not a follower of Christ, said, "Truly this man was the Son of God" (Mark 15:39).

From His start as a tiny baby born in Bethlehem, Jesus progressed through boyhood, to manhood, and finally to godhood. He was the most noble and holy Being who ever lived upon this earth. In just three years' time He accomplished countless miracles, preached never-ending eternal doctrines, and forever altered the souls of men and women who followed Him. But the question remains: Do people in today's world still allow Jesus inside their lives to change their souls? Nothing can be more important— no other crusade is more vital. Those who now reside on earth, collectively and individually, need peace—eternal, everlasting peace, which comes only through the gospel of Jesus Christ. Peace and pride cannot co-exist. Only the humble and penitent will receive the peace of Christ, who overcame the world.

Grow toward Godliness

Growing old is unavoidable. Growing up is optional. Growing toward godliness is an absolute. That is, unless you'd rather grow toward wickedness. Perhaps endless torment amid fire and brimstone appeals to you. I personally prefer an air-conditioned setting in which to live eternally

Our lives are meant to overflow with joy, love, peace, truth, and other heaven-sent virtues. However, this doesn't mean we'll be free from afflictions, for even the sinless Jesus did not escape earthly trials. Yet in the midst of forging through hardships, He grew toward maturity and Godhood. Jesus was required to "suffer temptations, and pain of body, hunger thirst, and fatigue, even more than a man can suffer, except it be unto death;" (Mosiah 3:7). Though we're not asked to endure agony equal to Christ's, each tribulation we confront and conquer will hone our souls and make us more like Him.

Each of us… needs to reach down into the innermost recesses of our souls to find the divinity that is deep within us and to earnestly petition the Lord for an endowment of special wisdom and inspiration. Only when we so profoundly reach the depths of our beings can we discover our true identity, our self-worth, and our purpose in life. Only as we seek to be purged of selfishness and of concern for recognition and wealth can we find some sweet relief from the anxieties, hurts, pains, miseries, and concerns of this world (James E. Faust, "Heirs to the Kingdom of God," *Ensign*, May 1995, 63).

It has been said that life is a grindstone; whether it grinds you down, or polishes you up, depends on your attitude and perceptions. That corresponds with a Chinese proverb: "A gem cannot be polished without friction. Neither can a man or woman gain wisdom without trials." Just as our fingerprints differ, our tribulations will range from short and sweet to dramatic and traumatic. This is according to our Father's plan for each individual.

Though it may not seem so at the time, our agony will be minuscule compared to what Christ endured on Calvary's cross—particularly at the moment God the Father withdrew, leaving Jesus to face His anguish alone. That will not happen to us. It's not in God's nature to let us suffer alone.

> No matter how serious the trial, how deep the distress, how great the affliction, [God] will never desert us. He never has, and He never will. He cannot do it. It is not His character. He is an unchangeable being;... [and] we have made Him our friend, by obeying His Gospel; and He will stand by us. We may pass through the fiery furnace; we may pass through deep waters; but we shall not be consumed nor overwhelmed. We shall emerge from all these trials and difficulties the better and purer for them, if we only trust in our God, and keep His commandments. [George Q. Cannon, *Collected Discourses* 2:185, 121.]

Our wise Father knows that adversity makes His children both strong and humble. He has promised to faithfully rescue us: "There hath no temptation taken you but such as is common to man: but God is faithful, who will not suffer you to be tempted above that ye are able; but will with the temptation also make a way to escape, that ye may be able to bear it" (1 Corinthians 10:13).

No pain that we suffer, no trial that we experience is wasted. It ministers to our education, to the development of such qualities as patience, faith, fortitude, and humility. All that we suffer and all that we endure, especially when we endure it patiently, builds up our characters, purifies our hearts, expands our souls, and makes us more tender and charitable,… which will make us more like our Father and Mother in heaven (Orson F. Whitney). [See Spencer W. Kimball, *Faith Precedes the Miracle*, Salt Lake City, Deseret Book Co., 1972, 98.]

Imagine evolving to be more like our Heavenly Parents! What greater blessings could we seek? This is the creme de la creme. And it even gets better! We're invited to live with Them eternally! Astounding! A trip to the moon has only been offered to a few select astronauts—and they could only stay a few days. Yet the invitation to live forever and ever in the celestial kingdom is extended to every worthy son and daughter of God.

Perfect and Sinless

Jesus, "being pure and spotless before God, could not look upon sin save it be with abhorrence" (Alma 13:12). Because He was perfect and sinless, He did not know the pain of weakness, worldliness, or wickedness. Nor had He felt how the consequences of sin break down human souls in temporal and spiritual ways.

Through the Spirit, Jesus understood the dredges of pain, evil, sin, and sorrow—especially on days when He empathized with those around Him. "Now the spirit knoweth all things; nevertheless the Son of God suffereth according to the flesh, that he might take upon him the sins of his people" (Alma 7:13). Until that fateful night in Gethsemane, Christ's physical body had remained pure and untarnished from deep pain and sorrow, for He had not yet received exacting knowledge through His flesh. But as He petitioned the Father, the agony stunned Him to the point that He began to "tremble because of pain, and to bleed at every pore" (D&C 19:18). Never before had Christ's physical body—His flesh and bones, nerves and brain, heart and blood—experienced such astronomical anguish.

In that fateful prayer, Jesus was burdened by every possible negative human thought and dreadful human feeling. Our Savior descended below every horrific human desire, each injurious abuse, and all excruciating evil acts. The powers of Hell thundered through Him. Darkness and despair enveloped Him as He fought to endure this unfathomable pit of pain and grief. What a battle must have ensued as the terror and humiliation of His humanness grappled against His divinity and Godly power! Perhaps for only a split second, His supernal spirit was held captive by His mortal soul. Then, like most who've lived on earth, Jesus yearned to shrink away from the repulsive bitter cup, and asked His Father to remove it. Not ever having experienced in the flesh such tormenting sin and sorrow, the Savior's torture was so tremendous that "there appeared an angel unto him from heaven, strengthening him" (Luke 22:43). The anguish was far more grotesque than He imagined— even with His supreme omniscience. Yet He courageously opposed all of Satan's tactics.

This was done to fulfill the Father's will. Now Jesus thoroughly comprehends—far more than any mortal—what each of us is called upon to endure. Jesus offers a portion of His redeeming power to release us from anguish, but only according to our faith in Him and our degree of penitence.

Jesus calls after us, "return unto me, and repent of your sins, and be converted, that I may heal you" (3 Nephi 9:13). After we confess and forsake our iniquities, the Lord, will "remember them no more" (D&C 58:42).

Conclusion

We are dependent on our Savior's Atonement to ransom us, for we cannot achieve salvation without the Redeemer's priceless gift to us. In return, perhaps we should become more like Jesus Christ—one step at a time, one simple act to lift another soul, one little sacrifice to become more humble, one small display of love and compassion, one uttered prayer of gratitude, and one courageous move toward enhanced spirituality.

> [Jesus] offered to use his bounty to pay for our folly [with] his infinite perfection to compensate for our countless mistakes. He offered to do so at a price of pain beyond calculation or imagination....
>
> The feelings unlocked in us by that condescension went beyond anything we had ever known. The generosity and power of the offered atonement filled us with awe. He who owed us nothing would give us everything. At the cost of unimaginable personal suffering, he would use his endless credits to balance our endless debits. He would give himself as a ransom in the ultimate act of love. [Richard Eyre, *Life Before Life*, Salt Lake City, Deseret Book Co., 1999, 104–6.]

Because of the inestimable love Jesus has for us, He sacrificed His very life so we might receive exaltation. This was not blind submission to the Father. Our Redeemer chose to be obedient, saying, "Therefore doth my Father love me, because I lay down my life, that I may take it again. No man taketh it from me, but I lay it down of myself. I have power to lay it down, and I have power to take it again. This commandment have I received of my Father" (John 10:17–18).

We, too, can symbolically lay down our lives by sacrificing our time, talents, intellects, and energy for the sake of others and to build God's kingdom. With the power of our agency, we can choose to obey, sacrifice, and humbly submit to the will of our Father.

As mortals, we have imperfect perception. Therefore, we might view the pathway to eternal life as a steep climb—like hiking with a heavy backpack to the top of a high Himalayan peak. Yet if we walk beside the Lord, I testify that any mountains we confront in life—whether imaginary or real—can be surmounted. I've learned that it is in the toil and struggle of climbing heavenward that our spiritual muscles become taut and strong. As Susan Ames sang in a song she wrote:

> *Give me this mountain, I want to climb it.*
> *I want the sun [Son] to shine upon my face.*
> *Give me this mountain, Lord,*
> *It will be my saving grace."*
> ["Give Me this Mountain," Jentle Jungle Productions, Providence, UT, 1992.]

Surely, it is through adversity, travail, and sacrifice that we are intimately connected with Jesus Christ, and thus, become more like Him.

As for me, I will behold thy face in righteousness: I shall be satisfied, when I awake, with thy likeness (Psalms 17:15).

For additional insight see:
Elaine A. Cannon, *Adversity*, Salt Lake City, Bookcraft, 1987.

.

Wherefore my beloved brethren,
pray unto the Father with all the energy of heart,
that ye may be filled with this love....
that when he shall appear we shall be like him,
for we shall see him as he is;
Moroni 7:48

We Shall Be Like Him

It has been said that "God sent Jesus to earth as love, so we could learn to love as Jesus." Those who desire to become purified and like Him must "pray unto the Father with all the energy of heart, that [we] may be filled" with the pure love of Christ (see Moroni 7:47–48). These verses are from a sermon Mormon preached about faith, hope, and charity. These three principles each connect us with Jesus Christ: "faith in Christ" (v. 39), "hope through the atonement of Christ" (v. 41) and charity "the pure love of Christ" (v. 47).

Both Alma the Younger and Joseph Smith emphasized that faith, hope, and charity are not idle principles. To be fully effective these qualities must be combined with work, meaning that action and effort are involved. "And see that ye have faith, hope, and charity, and then ye will always abound in good works" (Alma 7:24). There are no unemployment benefits for those who fail to abound in good works. Couch potatoes need not apply for this glorious work. The qualifications are simple in scope, yet profound. "And faith, hope, charity and love, with an eye single to the glory of God, qualify him for the work" (D&C 4:5).

Most of us are familiar with Apostle Paul's treatise on charity, with which he closes, "And now abideth faith, hope, charity, these three; but the greatest of these is charity" (1 Corinthians 13:13). Perhaps charity is the greatest of these three principles because it was through the pure love of Christ that He wrought the infinite Atonement.

> Jesus and His Atonement represent the most profound expression of Heavenly Father's love for His children.... Our gratitude for Christ and His Atonement will grow with the years and the decades. It will never cease growing, for the scriptures foretell that we will praise Him for ever and ever. [Neal A. Maxwell, spoken at missionary satellite conference Aug. 29, 1999, *LDS Church News*, Sept. 4, 1999, 5.]

Pure Love

To eventually emulate the pure love of Christ, we should practice using it every single day. In bygone years, teachers made wayward students write down their inadequacies a hundred times on the blackboard. However, writing "Love One Another," one hundred times won't be beneficial in learning to love in a Christlike manner. As the poet Chanh Kha wrote, "Love wasn't put in the heart to stay, for love isn't love 'til you give it away."

Love requires active efforts of compassion, mercy, kindness, and benevolence. Forgiveness is also a key ingredient of love, as Jesus said from the cross, "Father forgive them; for they know not what they do" (Luke 23:34). Like Christ, we should never prejudge people who don't have the knowledge necessary to live the gospel. "The nearer we get to our Heavenly Father, the more we are disposed to look with compassion on perishing souls; we feel that we want to take them upon our shoulders, and cast their sins behind our backs.... If you would have God have mercy on you, have mercy on one another" [*Teachings of the Prophet Joseph Smith*, 240–241.]

Often, the question in dealing with others is not *what should I DO*, but rather *what shall I BE?* The answer never varies from "be like Him." Amid this unsettling world, I must settle my heart on the pure love of Christ—not just occasionally, but "at all times and in all things, and in all places that [I] may be in, even until death" (Mosiah 18:9). As the familiar saying goes, "Live in such a way that those who know you but don't know Christ will want to know Christ because they know you."

Always Have His Spirit

During each Sunday's sacrament service, we covenant to "always remember him and keep his commandments," that we may "always have his spirit to be with [us]" (D&C 20:77). What a magnificent blessing to always have Spirit of the Lord!

When you draw near to Jesus Christ, His Spirit will quietly dwell in your soul. With His scarred feet, He will walk softly by your side. If you reach toward Him, He will gently take your hand in His, and you would feel His wounded palm press against yours. He has promised, "Yet will I not forget thee. Behold, I have graven thee upon the palms of my hands" (Isaiah 19:15–16). Our Savior never forgets us. From eternity to eternity, we are uppermost in His thoughts.

Those who keep Christ in remembrance will receive peace in their souls, particularly during these stressful last days. Many of us recall the tragedies of September 11, 2001, when terrorist pilots hijacked four airplanes filled with innocent passengers. Though one plane missed its target and crashed in a field, two veered into the World Trade Towers in New York, and the fourth hit the Pentagon in Washington, D.C. That was a crucial point in history, which threatened the security of the United States, as did events such as the attack on Pearl Harbor in 1941 and the assassination of President John F. Kennedy in 1963.

Since the earth's genesis, both good and evil have rippled through nations to either uplift humans or cause their downfall—depending on their reactions. In these latter days, the world has experienced an increase of wars, tsunamis, famines, earthquakes, diseases, hurricanes, and various other heart-wrenching disasters. When tragedy strikes, it's necessary to respond with vigor and with faith. After a tornado, the cleanup requires more than emptying the kitchen wastebasket. Each catastrophe demands special attention and tools.

To illustrate in a minor way, I recall a day when the drain from our bathroom sink began to back up. I simply used a plunger, and quickly dislodged three pennies that someone—surely, not my perfect grandchildren—had let slip down the drain. On another occasion, I accidentally clogged our kitchen drain by putting too many re-hydrated peas from our food storage in the disposal. It required far more than a plunger or Draino or Liquid Plumber to remedy the situation. We had to call in a plumber with an industrial-sized auger to snake through the pipes and cleanse them. Now that was a costly repair!

When any disaster occurs from minor home calamities to something of worldwide significance, many people reach out to both give and receive aid. With instantaneous media around the world, we hear heart-warming stories of humanitarian efforts offered by individuals or organizations, like the Red Cross. The LDS Church also provides countless services to improve conditions, whether caused by calamities or impoverished living: medical supplies and personnel to aid victims, voluntary work crews to clean ravaged areas, wells drilled to provide clean water, tent cities or huts built for temporary housing, vaccinations against childhood diseases, clothing, blankets, and sanitary supplies shipped to those in need, and so on.

No matter the cause of adversity—whether individual or global—and no matter the source of assistance to relieve the hardship, it's important to remember the Lord is aware of the tragedy. Through the Spirit, He will send peace amid conflict to those who draw near to Him. Remember that any catastrophe we confront may seem enormous at the time, yet it is minor in comparison to our Savior's atonement on the cross for all the griefs and pains of the world. When we are true to our covenants, the Lord will respond by providing an added measure of strength so we might endure to the end. "I, the Lord, am bound when ye

do what I say; but when ye do not what I say, ye have no promise"
(D&C 82:10).

There are few people in these latter-days who have suffered
more affliction and persecution than Joseph Smith. Amid the
Prophet's merciless imprisonment in Liberty Jail, the Lord spoke
these comforting words:

> My son, peace be unto thy soul; thine adversity and thine
> afflictions shall be but a small moment;
>
> And then, if thou endure it well, God shall exalt thee on
> high. (D&C 121:7–8).
>
> … know thou, my son, that all these things shall give thee
> experience, and shall be for thy good.
>
> The Son of Man hath descended below them all. Art thou
> greater than he? (D&C 122:7–8).

Putting Christ's Sacrifice in Perspective

The Bible records many millennia of events. Some of these are
of monumental importance: the creation of the world, the fall of
Adam and Eve, Moses rescuing the Israelites from bondage, Lehi
leaving Jerusalem with his family, and the birth of Jesus. Yet in all
this world's history, there has been but one significant phenomenon
upon which our salvation teeters: the Atonement of Christ. When
our Father's eternal plan of salvation required a Savior, Jesus
volunteered for this sacred, yet disquieting, crucifixion.

All creation is founded upon the Lord's willingness to die that
we might be resurrected and spiritually reborn. Every chronicled
event on this planet—ancient or modern—is put into proper
perspective by His infinite sacrifice in the meridian of time. Each
minute, hour, week, and year of this earth's existence has been to
perpetuate life for the children of God—not just in this world, but
in the eternal realms ahead.

For centuries, prophets have targeted the Savior's selfless,
sacrificial Atonement as the premier theme around which all the
gospel rotates. Nothing else in history matters. The focal point
of all scripture is riveted on Christ's forfeiting His comfort to

be nailed upon the cross. Even the life of Jesus pivots upon this excruciating, yet colossal, act of compassion. Nothing on earth compares in magnanimity and eternal scope to what our Redeemer did for us. Whether people realize it or not, everyone that has been born—or is yet to be born—is dependent upon the Atonement and resurrection of our Lord, Jehovah. Salvation and exaltation are mere dreams without this foremost component of doctrine.

As John the Beloved wrote, "Worthy is the Lamb that was slain, to receive power, and riches, and wisdom, and strength, and honor, and glory, and blessing" (Revelation 5:12). What a hallowed opportunity when we testify to others of this monumental deed! How sacred is our task to bring each soul on earth to Christ! With His sublime example to follow, and His Spirit to light our way, we cannot fail.

> Behold, I am the light; I have set an example for you.
>
> Therefore, hold up your light that it may shine unto the world. Behold, I am the light which ye shall hold up—that which ye have seen me do....
>
> And ye see that I have commanded that none of you should go away, but rather have commanded that ye should come unto me, that ye might feel and see; even so shall ye do unto the world (3 Nephi 18:16, 24, 25).

Become Saviors

Each child of God can play an important role to assist our Savior in bringing salvation to all the world. Just as our Father sent His Son to redeem men and women from their weaknesses, He has entrusted us with a similar mission to save one another.

> We came here to be saviors. "What, saviors?" "Yes." "Why we thought there was only one Savior." "Oh, yes, there are a great many. What do the scriptures say about it?" One of the old prophets, in speaking of these things, says that saviors shall come up upon Mount Zion (see Obadiah 1:21). Saviors? Yes. Whom shall they save? In the first place themselves, then

their families, then their neighbors, friends, and associations, then their forefathers, then pour blessings on their posterity. Is that so? Yes. [John Taylor, *Deseret News: Semi-Weekly*, 11 Feb. 1873, 2.]

Since we shouted with joy for the chance to come to earth, we should continue rejoicing as we take part in this work and glory "to bring to pass the immortality and eternal life of man" (Moses 1:39). No disputing, it is work! Remember Snow White, who taught the seven dwarfs to "Whistle While You Work"? That's a great idea—for those who know how to whistle. Or there are plenty of hymns to sing, with motivating words, such as, "let us all press on in the work of the Lord," and "we all have work, let no one shirk, put you shoulder to the wheel," and "sweet is the work." The point is that God's work is never-ending. Our individual labors are essential to fulfill the purposes of the Father.

Jesus had not finished his work when his body was slain, neither did he finish it after his resurrection from the dead; although he had accomplished the purpose for which he then came to the earth, he had not yet fulfilled all his work. And when will he? Not until he has redeemed and saved every son and daughter of our father Adam that have been or ever will be born upon this earth to the end of time, except the sons of perdition. That is his mission. We will not finish our work until we have saved ourselves, and then not until we shall have saved all depending upon us; for we are to become saviors upon Mount Zion, as well as Christ. We are called to this mission. [Joseph F. Smith, *Gospel Doctrine*, 442.]

Testimony of Jesus Christ

In this books' prologue, I described a day at the Garden Tomb, which reinforced my testimony of Jesus Christ. I know He lives and will exist through all eternity. He is my Savior. He is your Savior. It is not required to journey to faraway places, like Israel, in order to enrich one's testimony of our Redeemer. However, it is crucial to know for oneself the reality of the Messiah and His infinite atonement. Those truths will enhance our motivation to become more like Christ. It doesn't require a Sabbath fast and testimony meeting for us to bear witness of the Lord. We should testify frequently and without shame, when an opportunity presents itself. "For whosoever shall be ashamed of me and my word, of him shall the Son of Man be ashamed" (Luke 9:26). "Be not thou therefore ashamed of the testimony of our Lord" (2 Timothy 1:8).

Last summer, I was driving while three of my grandsons sat in the back seat and sang along with a children's station on the satellite radio. The chorus of one song repeated, "We don't know where we came from…. We have the whole universe, and it's ours." From the backseat came the confident statement of an eight-year-old boy, "Some of us know where we came from." Though he'd been baptized less than a year, this boy affirmed that he'd been sent to earth from our heavenly home. He knew his divine origin as a child of God. What a testimony builder for me to hear his innocent witness of truth! Is it any wonder that Jesus proclaimed, "Suffer little children, and forbid them not, to come unto me: for of such is the kingdom of heaven" (Matthew 19:4). Jesus also said, "Except ye be converted, and become as little children, ye shall not enter into the kingdom of heaven" (Matthew 18:3).

How difficult it is for adults to maintain a childlike and humble perspective about life! Perhaps we'd have a better chance of stability if we could skip over adolescence, which is often fraught with Satan's snares. Come to think of it, I'd prefer to avoid a few other stages of life—like that time… oh, never mind. Perhaps you have a few regrets, too.

We're blessed to live in a day and age when testimonies from Church leaders are carried throughout the world by television, radio, internet, satellite transmissions, and printed media. The First Presidency and Twelve Apostles are ordained as "special witnesses of the name of Christ in all the world" (D&C 107:23). Their testimonies include bearing witness of His bodily resurrection from the dead. This means each apostle receives a touch of the Divine from beyond the veil of this earth—though rarely are such sacred events shared in public. Consider this vibrant witness from Elder Melvin J. Ballard:

On this Easter day, we rejoice therefore not only in the testimony of those who saw and bore witness of the resurrection of Christ, but also that he still lives, the same resurrected being, and is the Savior of the world, that he still is planning for man's eternal salvation, and redemption, that he has visited the earth in this age, and that he is presently to come again, to dwell upon it with men for a thousand years.

I know as well as the doubting Thomas knew—when he had handled Christ and felt the prints of the nails in his hands and in his feet, all doubt was gone—I know as he knew, that Jesus is the Christ, that he is a reality. [Bryant S. Hinckley, *Sermons and Missionary Services of Melvin J. Ballard*, 275.]

In the eternities ahead, "every knee shall bow, and every tongue confess before him" (Mosiah 27:31). What a blessed event to fall on our knees and gaze up into His gentle face! How might we feel to see the nail prints in His hands, wrists, and feet? Imagine reaching out to touch His side that was pierced by a sword!

At times I wonder how my life might change if in this mortal world I could have just one glimpse of my Redeemer. Would I serve more diligently, show more compassion, manifest more faith and hope, be more humble and penitent, work harder to purify my life, and render more love to those around me? I hope so. Yet, even without a personal face-to-face encounter, I know Jesus lives, that He is real, and that He extends His pure love toward me. Therefore, I should not be taking baby steps, but giant leaps, to increase my faith and become more like Christ.

Faith to Move Water, Not Mountains

Years ago, I was enlightened by an experience that helped me better understand the Atonement of Christ. The day began with my driving up Weber Canyon to our family cabin, where I would chaperone a group of forty college-aged women in an overnight retreat. I relished my time as an adviser to Xi chapter of the LDS sorority, Lambda Delta Sigma, and I was glad the Xi officers had organized this outing. Though laughter, games, and late-night chatter would be part of the activities, these college girls especially wanted to share testimonies after dinner.

This was the first weekend in May, which meant that after leaving the asphalt highway, the dirt road to the cabin area would be closed due to thick mud and melting snow. From where I parked, it was an eighth of a mile walk to the cabin. Emptying my car of food and other supplies required carrying successive loads across a broad meadow then up the slope to our cabin.

The next task was to turn on the outside valve which would allow water into the cabin after its winter dormancy. In the basement, I located the long T-shaped tool, then I took it outside and lowered it into a four-foot hole. I rotated the valve and listened for a surge of water. But I heard nothing. Even so, I put away the T-bar and went to open the water valve inside the cabin. Not the slightest trickle came from any of the taps—only the hollow sound of air in the pipes.

Back outside, I checked the hand-pump, which usually brought a gush of water. Still nothing. At first, I thought the water might simply have disappeared from our cabin plumbing, meaning that this might not be a universal problem for all the cabins on the mountainside. I trudged downslope to the nearest cabin and tried its outside pump. Again, nothing but a hiss of air came through the pipes.

It was now 4:00 p.m. and the first sorority girls were due to arrive at 5:30, which meant they'd soon leave their homes in Salt Lake to make the hour-long drive. With haste, I went back inside my cabin and called my husband, Glenn, at his work. I asked if he knew anything about the water system being turned off. He said he'd make a few calls to other cabin owners and see what he could discover. While awaiting his reply, I phoned the Xi sorority president to explain the difficulty of not having water. Her immediate and apropos response was that we should petition the Lord for help, then call her back in a while. I hung up the phone and dropped to my knees with a hefty plea for Divine assistance. I implored the Lord to ask for His help—not for my sake, but for these sorority girls, who would to be spiritually edified with our testimony sharing. Though all the pipes around me seemed empty of moisture, my tears flowed freely. I determined if faith as small as a grain of mustard seed could move mountains, then I must exhibit adequate faith to move water.

Ten minutes later, Glenn phoned to say the directors of the cabin association had been working on the water lines, and the system was still turned off. One man was due to come Saturday morning and restore the flow of water, but that wouldn't help me tonight with a cabin full of college girls.

Glenn offered to leave his job and drive up to remedy the problem, if I was willing to do some legwork in the meantime. My job was to go in search of the tool needed to turn on the major water valve to all the cabins. As I understood it, this would be a T-bar, similar to the one I'd used to turn on the valve outside our cabin. However, this T-bar was thicker in diameter and made of iron or steel. Glenn provided only two clues for finding the water main T-bar: It was supposedly propped up outside a cabin on Sunrise Lane, and the name on the cabin started with "W." I knew that Sunrise Lane was the half-mile loop sweeping the highest arc on the mountainside. It would be an uphill climb to reach that lane, then I'd have to circle ten or twelve cabins until I found the tool. But in my sturdy hiking boots, I felt "woman enough" for the task.

Though I'd pre-prayed, I wasn't fully prepared. I hadn't expected the snow to increase in depth the higher I hiked on the mountainside. Under the snow, the road was muddy and slippery, making my knees and ankles twist awkwardly with each step. My breathing became ragged with the uphill climb. Finally reaching Sunrise Lane, I carefully circled each cabin to look for a "W," marking the one with the T-bar propped outside. I searched everywhere possible: in carports, beside woodpiles, around wooden decks, and under picnic tables and benches. None of the ten cabins on my circuit were marked by a name starting with "W," nor did they offered up the treasure for which I searched. Arriving again at the bottom of the lane, I exhaled a hopeless breath of air. My shoulders drooped in despair because my mission had been fruitless. My boots and socks were soaked with muddy slime, my knees and ankles ached from the unsteady gait, and my energy waned. Unfortunately, my faith had also diminished.

I now had two choices: to give up my search, or to once again traverse the snowy loop. I chose the latter. My legs tried to protest as I trudged up the lane and slowly circled the first six cabins. Only four more cabins stood along the downhill stretch. I circled two with no success. The speck of faith that remained in me said it was useless to continue. I guess a speck is smaller than a mustard seed, but not by much. Shaking my head in doubt, I raised my arms in the air to signal giving up.

That's when I recalled a thought that hangs on the wall in my home office: "Those who see the hand of God in everything can best leave everything in God's hands." Though distressed and fatigued, I knew God was omniscient, and if it was His will, He could solve the mystery of the missing T-bar. Gazing heavenward, I prayed aloud, "Heavenly Father, I don't want to give up. But I'm only human. I can't view the earth from your heavenly perspective. Please, wilt Thou help me find the T-bar? I can't do this alone."

The quick prayer restored my faith, and I moved toward the next cabin. When I started down the lengthy driveway to go around the cabin, my eyes suddenly spied the T-bar. It was supposed to be propped against the cabin, but it had fallen over in a bank of snow. That's why I'd missed seeing it in my initial search.

Gratitude flooded my soul, and I breathed a prayer of thanks. Then I raced forward to free the T-bar from the mound of snow. However, it did not rise easily—the tool was much heavier than I expected. Made of thick iron pipes nearly three inches in diameter, the top of the T was four feet long, attached to a five-foot stem. The only way I could hoist it was to lay the T-bar over my right shoulder and let the stem drag on the ground. Then I slowly tugged it up the driveway to the snow-covered lane.

I felt some relief in knowing my trek back to my cabin was along either downhill or flat lanes—otherwise my strength would fail. A glance at my watch said it was 5:15, and Glenn should arrive at our cabin any minute. The sorority girls were also due soon, but I hoped they'd run late, as was their usual timing. With the sizable T-bar resting on one shoulder and the stem bumping against my spine, I could manage only a slow gait through the snow and mud. My already-sore knees took the brunt of the T-bar's added weight.

After a time, I paused to catch my breath and re-adjust how I held the T-bar. As I grasped the upper bar and laid it across my left shoulder, a sudden scene flashed in my mind. I recalled a movie of Christ struggling to drag His cross through the streets of Jerusalem. Though in reality He probably carried just the upper beam, many movies portray the entire cross to add trauma and drama. I envisioned the Savior bowed beneath the load as agony marred His countenance. I saw His faltering steps as cruel soldiers thrust Him forward. Throngs of people in the crowded streets badgered Jesus with unkind words.

The T-bar I carried seemed suddenly like a cross. Though my load could not in the least equal the burdens Jesus bore for the sins of the world, I could identify with His journey toward Golgotha. As I struggled to drag the T-bar through the snowy forest, I imagined each tree as a person deriding my progress. Yet each step I took meant I could soon provide water for the sorority girls— just as Christ offers living water, "springing up into everlasting life" (see John 4:11–14). What a staggering comparison!

More than ever before, I understood the meaning of our Savior's infinite sacrifice and why He had willingly given His life. Tears pooled in my eyes. I had to stop walking so I wouldn't fall on the slippery slope. This T-bar, laid on my shoulder was indeed a burden, but I bore it nobly and valiantly, as Jesus had done. Nothing could persuade me to lay aside this challenge, for it would bless many lives, if I could endure with patience.

It didn't matter that my hands ached from their cold, tight grip on the iron pipe. Indescribable love thundered through me.

The Lord had graciously shouldered my iniquities and afflictions, my griefs, sorrows, and pains. Only through His Atonement, could I obtain eternal life. Carrying this cross-like tool was the least I could do in return.

In a profound way, I comprehended Christ's willingness to suffer for the sake of others. No matter how intense my travail, I knew I would endure anything for the salvation of these college girls. I loved each one dearly, as if I'd given birth to them like my own daughter. Whatever God required of me to bring redemption to His children, I would diligently do it with all my heart, might, mind, and strength. Even giving my own life would not seem too heavy a price. That's what Jesus did for me.

Through grace, salvation can be attained by all our Father's children. It didn't matter to Jesus what price He might pay to atone for us. Neither should the cost matter to me. I should willingly consecrate my time, talents, energy—and everything else with which I've been blessed—to bring others unto Christ so He can save them in the kingdom of our Father.

I soon completed the trek back to our cabin, where my husband had just arrived. Glenn took the T-bar off my shoulder and gave me a look of wonder for carrying it as far as I had.

Within fifteen minutes, water surged anew through the pipes on the mountainside and into our cabin. Ten more minutes passed, and the first batch of sorority girls arrived for our overnight retreat.

Later that evening, I stood before them and shared how my speck of faith, smaller than a mustard seed, had been strong enough to move water. Only through heaven-sent blessings could I have accomplished the task. I testified how carrying the T-bar had increased my comprehension of the Lord's anguished efforts to save the world from pain and sin. In taking up my cross to follow Him, I came to know the Savior in a far more personal way.

Conclusion

Heavenly Father and Jesus Christ know us intimately—our joys and sorrows, our fears and triumphs. They have embraced us with unfathomable love. We can become like the Father and the Son by cultivating characteristics of godliness. They expect great victory as we utilize Their divine power in these latter days, as revealed to Nephi: "And it came to pass that I, Nephi, beheld the power of the Lamb of God, that it descended upon the saints of the church of the Lamb, and upon the covenant people of the Lord, who were scattered upon all the face of the earth; and they were armed with righteousness and with the power of God in great glory" (1 Nephi 14:14).

I testify that Jesus Christ is the Messiah, who sacrificed His life to atone for all our Father's children. Our Redeemer now reigns as King of Kings and Lord of Lords in heavenly realms. Someday, He will return to rule personally upon the earth.

I wonder, do I know Christ well enough to recognize Him when He appears? Are my highest goals in life to learn of Him and become like Him? Do I worship Him? Study His teachings? Heed His words? Hope in His mercy? Seek His love? Feel the peace He offers? Rejoice in Him? Prepare the world to receive Him?

From the evening of birth, when there was no room for Jesus to be born at the inn, to the present days when people question if there is room in their hearts to be born again in His name, the Messiah offers peace to those who come unto Him.

From the first moment of life, when Jesus was tenderly coddled and wrapped in swaddling clothes, to His last day of life when He was brutally stripped of His clothing and nailed upon the cross, our Redeemer set an example of humility.

From the tender night, when nurturing parents laid Jesus in a manger, to His agonizing death when devoted friends laid Him in a tomb, the Savior sacrificed His entire life to do the Father's will.

From His first feeble cries in a lowly stable, to His soul-wrenching prayer in Gethsemane, Christ's voice beckons us to follow Him toward eternity. [Written by the author for a lesson in 1993.]

May we always, always remember that Christ has atoned for us through His pure love. And may every child of God, "pray unto the Father will all the energy of heart, that [we] may be filled with this love,... that when [Christ] shall appear we shall be like him" (Moroni 7:48).

For additional insight see:
Bruce R. McConkie, "The Purifying Power of Gethsemane," *Ensign*, May 1985, 9 - 11.
Doctrine and Covenants 76:50-70.

Appendix
Bibliography

Benson, Ezra Taft. *The Teachings of Ezra Taft Benson*. Salt Lake City, Bookcraft, 1988.

Cannon, George Q. *Collected Discourses, Vol 2*. Salt Lake City.

Children's Songbook. Salt Lake City. The Church of Jesus Christ of Latter-day Saints, 1989.

Eyre, Richard. *Life Before Life*. Salt Lake City, Deseret Book Co., 1999.

Holy Bible, Authorized King James Version. Salt Lake City, The Church of Jesus Christ of Latter-day Saints, 1979.

Hymns of The Church of Jesus Christ of Latter-day Saints. Salt Lake City, The Church of Jesus Christ of Latter-day Saints, 1985.

Kimball, Spencer W. *Faith Precedes the Miracle*. Salt Lake City, Deseret Book Co, 1972.

Kimball, Spencer W. *The Teachings of Spencer W. Kimball, ed. by Edward L. Kimball*. Salt Lake City, Bookcraft, 1982.

Lee, Harold B. *Teachings of Harold B. Lee*. Salt Lake City, Bookcraft, 1996.

Ludlow, Victor. *Principles and Practices of the Restored Gospel*. Salt Lake City, Deseret Book Co., 1992.

Lundwall, N. B. *Temples of the Most High God.* Salt Lake City, Bookcraft.

McKay, David O. *Ancient Apostles.* Salt Lake City, Deseret Book Co., 1964.

Millet, Robert L, *Alive in Christ: The Miracle of Spiritual Rebirth.* Salt Lake City, Deseret Book, 1997.

Smith, Joseph. *History of the Church.* Salt Lake City, Deseret Book Co, 1978.

Smith, Joseph. *Lectures on Faith.* Salt Lake City, Deseret Book Co., 1985.

Smith, Joseph, translator. *The Book of Mormon.* Salt Lake City, The Church of Jesus Christ of Latter-day Saints, 1981.

Smith, Joseph. *The Doctrine and Covenants.* Salt Lake City, The Church of Jesus Christ of Latter-day Saints, 1981.

Smith, Joseph. *The Pearl of Great Price.* Salt Lake City, The Church of Jesus Christ of Latter-day Saints, 1981.

Smith, Joseph. *Teachings of the Prophet Joseph Smith,* sel. by Joseph Fielding Smith, Salt Lake City, Deseret Book Co., 1976.

Smith, Joseph F. *Collected Discourses Delivered by President Wilford Woodruff, His Two Counselors, the Twelve Apostles, and Others,* Vol. 4. Salt Lake City.

Smith, Joseph F. *Gospel Doctrine, 5th Edition.* Salt Lake City, Deseret Book Co.,1939.

Smith, Joseph F. *The Origin of Man by the First Presidency of the Church.*

Taylor, John. *Teachings of the Presidents of the Church: John Taylor.* Salt Lake City, 2001.

Young, Brigham. *Discourses of Brigham Young, vol. 9 & 10* arranged by John A. Widtsoe. Salt Lake City, Deseret Book, 1954.

Appendix
Index

A

Abraham 27, 33-34, 64

adversity 8, 19, 33, 44, 63, 74, 127, 133, 137, 142, 143

agency 13, 52, 74, 103, 136

always remember Him 41, 118, 154

anchor 11, 69

aspen trees 11

Atonement 15, 24, 32, 55, 77, 93, 94, 96-99, 118-119, 122, 126, 135, 140, 143-144, 147, 152

attributes of godliness 3, 28, 102, 105

B

Ballard, Melvin J. 147

become one 2-3, 15, 42, 108

Benson, Ezra Taft 52, 69-70

black and white 38-39

blind 68, 70-71, 97, 121, 130, 136

bread crumbs 122

brother of Jared 43-45

C

Calvary 96, 99, 101, 133

Cannon, George Q. 133

celestial homesickness 114

change 2, 69-70, 121, 126, 132, 147

charity 101, 105, 118, 139, 140

cherry tree 109

child of God, children of God, 28, 32, 77, 89, 101, 107, 127, 143-144, 146, 154

Christ 1, 3, 11-12, 14-15, 17-27, 29-33, 36-38, 40-42, 45, 47, 49, 53-58, 60-65, 68-71, 75-87, 89, 91-97, 99-101, 103-104, 106-107, 112-113, 118-128, 131-137, 139-141, 143-147, 151-154

cliff story 4-11

clones 2

Creator 10, 78, 88

crown of glory 111-113

D

dedication of temples 55, 56
disasters 141-142
dispensation of the fulness of times 17-18
doubt 53, 62, 100, 147

E

Einstein 64, 78
Elijah 4, 65
emulate Christ 15, 106, 126, 128, 105, 140
endure 10, 15, 37, 86, 110, 114, 118, 123, 132, 134-135, 142-143, 151-152
endure to the end 15, 118, 142
Enoch 18, 64, 88, 101, 102, 103
eternal life 11, 14, 19, 25, 32, 36, 40, 45, 62, 64, 82, 94-95, 103, 112, 120-121, 136, 145, 152
eternal perspective 4, 11-12, 49, 88
eternity 4, 19, 34, 37, 60, 79, 82, 91-93, 95, 108, 121, 123, 141, 145, 153
exaltation 11, 13, 14, 32, 33, 52, 57, 59, 60, 95, 102, 106-107, 112-113, 127, 136, 144
example 14-15, 21, 32, 54-55, 60, 71, 78, 90, 97, 102, 105, 123, 127, 144, 153
eye single to the glory of God 121, 139
Eyre, Richard 136

F

faith 8, 10-13, 18-19, 21-22, 24, 31, 33-35, 37-38, 45, 60-71, 75-76, 81, 84-85, 87, 89, 91, 93, 97, 100-101, 103, 105, 110, 118, 121, 128, 130, 134-135, 139-140, 142, 147, 149, 150, 152
faith and works 34, 65, 75

faith to move wter 147
family 3, 6, 21, 37, 42-43, 47-48, 50, 51-53, 58-59, 65, 72, 75, 83, 85, 92, 114, 129, 143, 145, 147
Faust, James E 133
fear 6, 19, 25, 38, 61-62, 95, 98, 100, 101, 111, 113, 152
forgive, 97, 105, 140
fulness 17-23, 27-28, 30-31

G

Gethsemane 26, 54, 75, 96, 119, 126, 134, 153-154
Godhead 12-13
godliness 2, 4, 36-37, 51, 96, 102, 103, 105, 132, 153
God the Father, Heavenly Father 1, 3, 12, 14, 19, 21, 28, 35, 42, 45, 56-57, 71-72, 74, 77, 83, 87, 91, 93-96, 100, 102, 118-119, 127, 129, 133, 140, 150, 152
Golgotha 126, 151
good works 31, 65, 69, 106, 122, 139
grace for grace 20-22, 30, 31, 34, 43, 45, 50

H

heal, healed, healing, 24, 26, 55-56, 67-69, 70-71, 77, 97, 99-100, 114, 119, 130,135
hearts knit together 13
hike, hiking 5, 7, 10, 40, 50, 62, 79, 115. 136, 149
Hinckley, Gordon B. 58
Holland, Jeffrey R. 14, 124
holy, holiness 4, 29, 39, 45, 49-51, 53, 55-57, 69, 82, 87, 96, 102, 105, 111, 120, 122, 126, 128, 132
Holy Ghost, Holy Spirit 12-13, 18, 42, 62, 81, 90, 121
hope 9-10, 18, 27, 40, 52, 59, 62, 64, 69, 93, 103, 105, 111, 114, 117-118, 139, 140, 147

hospitalization 115-120

humanitarian 106, 142

humble 30, 35, 67, 80, 86, 119, 126,
128-129, 132-133, 136, 146,
147

humility 30, 80, 105, 134, 153

Hunter, Howard W. 58, 75, 76, 114

hymns and songs 14, 32, 40, 74, 118,
128, 131, 137, 146

I

intelligence 45-46, 92, 111, 123

J

Jerusalem 37, 47, 53, 68, 70, 130,
131, 143, 151

Jesus 1-3, 11-12, 14-15, 18-21, 23-
27, 29- 33, 37-38, 41-42, 45,
47-49, 53-56, 58, 60-63, 65-72,
75-77, 79-80, 83-84, 90-91, 93-
102, 104-108, 113, 118-123,
125-134, 136-137, 139-140,
141, 143-147, 151-153

joy 11, 18-19, 20, 27, 42, 51-52, 59,
72, 105, 118, 126, 128, 131-
132, 145

K

Kimball, Spencer W. 34, 112, 134

King Benjamin 18, 62, 80, 82

know God the Father and Jesus
Christ 21, 28, 111, 141, 147,
153

knowledge 1, 3, 27, 34, 41, 43, 59,
67, 78, 82, 89, 96, 105, 106,
111, 123, 128, 135, 140

L

last days 57, 141

latter days 14, 22, 55, 141, 153

Lazarus 93, 99

Lectures on Faith 42

Lee, Harold B 22, 57, 60

Lewis, C. S. 29, 42

life of Christ 128-132

light 12, 28, 30, 38, 40-44, 64, 71, 79,
82-84, 87, 89, 91-92, 99, 111-
112, 121-123, 127-128, 144

lightning 3-4

Light of Christ 40-41, 78, 83, 87, 121

light of truth 82, 92

like God the Father and Jesus Christ
12, 30 46, 92, 102-104, 119,
126, 132, 137, 139, 141, 146-
147,153

Longfellow, Henry Wadworth 35

love 3, 12-15, 32, 41, 45, 50-52, 60,
72, 77, 84, 92-95, 101-103,
105, 112, 119, 126, 132, 136,
139-141, 147, 151, 153-154

Ludlow, Victor 78, 92

M

Maxwell, Neal A. 15, 76, 94, 103,
104, 126, 140

McKay, David O. 90

mercy 3, 18, 32, 39, 57, 74, 96, 105,
107, 140, 153

mighty change of heart 2, 69, 120-
121, 126

Millet, Robert L. 120

miracles 10, 24, 38, 61-66, 69, 89, 97-
99, 101, 121, 123, 132

mission 2, 14, 15, 22, 34, 46, 49, 144,
145, 150

missionary 3, 4, 140

Moroni 37, 45, 62, 65, 69, 75, 81, 83,
95, 101, 139, 154

Moses 19, 35, 53, 64-65, 77-79, 83,
88, 91, 100-103, 127, 143, 145

mountains 5-6, 9, 44, 50, 52, 62, 66,
85, 99, 101, 136-137, 149

N

natural man 41, 119

nature 14, 40, 69, 70, 78, 84, 129, 133
neighbor 13, 30, 56, 92
Nelson, Russell M. 15, 104
nothing else in earth's history really matters except the atonement 143

O

oneness, be one 1-4, 8-10, 12-15, 17-18, 42, 78, 102, 106, 109, 114-115, 117, 121, 127, 129, 130-131, 136, 140-141, 143-147, 149, 151-152

P

Paul 13, 14, 38, 64, 140
peace 18, 33-34, 50-51, 58, 64, 68-69, 88, 93, 101, 105, 122, 126, 130-132, 141-143, 153
perfect 2-3, 15, 17, 45, 54, 88, 93, 95, 107, 108, 123, 134, 142
perfection 3, 4, 29, 107, 136
perspective 4, 9, 11, 12, 35, 49, 85, 88, 121, 143, 146, 150
Peter 23-27, 54-56, 76, 99, 100, 104
pine trees 4, 9-11
power 3, 20, 24, 34, 36, 38, 45-46, 50-52, 55-57, 60, 64-69, 71, 74-75, 81, 91-92, 96-98, 100-101, 107, 113, 119, 124, 127-128, 135-136, 144, 153-154
pray 15, 25, 45, 65, 67, 71-75, 95, 119, 139, 154
prayers 1, 10, 21, 35, 41, 43, 50, 51, 54-55, 63, 67-68, 71-76, 114, 118-119, 128, 135-136, 150, 153
pure 14, 39, 49, 56-57, 67, 87, 95, 101-102, 116, 119, 134, 139, 140-141, 147, 154
pure love 14, 95, 101-102, 139-141, 147, 154
purify 62, 69, 79, 147

R

repent 3, 20, 25, 36, 57, 66, 77, 135
repentance 31, 34, 39, 41, 79, 114
residue of the people 102
resurrection 18-19, 26-27, 36, 52, 67, 93-94, 99, 104, 107, 114, 123, 144-147
revelation 1, 29, 49, 50, 56, 68, 77, 110, 112
reverse 73
rewards 60, 64, 110-112, 126
rooted in Christ 11

S

sacrament 2, 21, 117-118, 141
sacrifice 14-15, 32, 53, 55, 58, 65, 95, 96, 99, 105, 120, 136-137, 143, 151
salvation 13, 20, 38, 39, 54, 60, 75, 80, 97, 111, 113, 122, 127, 131, 135, 143-144, 147, 152
sanctify 55, 88
Satan 4, 12, 25, 33-34, 39, 64, 81, 87, 94-96, 128, 135, 146
saviors, we can become 53, 144-145
Second Coming of Christ 58, 91, 125
sequoia tree 11, 36-37
sin cancer 114
Smith, Joseph 4, 17, 27, 29, 42, 78, 89-90, 106, 113, 122, 139-140, 143
Smith, Joseph F. 2-3, 12, 18, 28, 30, 46, 78, 106, 108, 145
Snow, Lorenzo 15, 22, 29, 52
substance of faith 12, 64, 92
sunflower 41
sun shine, Son shine 40-41

T

Talmage, James E. 115
taste the bitter 127
Taylor, John 92, 110-111, 145

Temple Square at Christmas 83
testimony 21, 22, 24, 27, 50, 85, 90-
    91, 145-147, 149
three years' ministry of Jesus 128
Thy will be done 76, 119
tornado 48, 66, 142
transfiguration 99
tree of life 38, 94
trust 38, 65, 69, 100, 126, 133
truth 1, 3, 13-14, 18, 20, 22, 29, 34,
    59, 77-78, 80-92, 128, 132, 146

U

unity 3, 12, 13, 105

V

virtues 3, 97, 104-105, 132

W

where we came from 146
Whitney, Orson F. 134
whole 13, 17, 45, 68-69, 78, 98, 121-
    122, 146
Widtsoe, John A. 50
wisdom 1, 35, 47-49, 72, 74, 84, 129,
    133, 144
Woodruff, Wilford 3, 56
work 23, 30-34, 46, 50-52, 55, 59-60,
    75, 89-90, 96, 102, 106, 110-
    113, 116-117, 119, 123, 139,
    142, 145, 147-148

Y

Young, Brigham 124

Z

Zion 79, 101-103, 107, 144, 145

About the Author
Bonnie Bradshaw Robinson

"Everyone in the ward wants you in their organization, including the Elders Quorum," said a bishop poised to issue a new calling to Bonnie. In the many ward and stake positions she has held, her favorites have been Young Women's camp director and advisor to the LDS Sorority, Lambda Delta Sigma, which led to a calling as the sorority's National Secretary

On a good day, Bonnie is compassionate, humorous, fearless, outdoorsy, energetic, and filled with faith. She's an avid reader, hiker, skier, and people watcher. Bonnie relishes time spent as a mother to four married children, grannie to nine grandchildren (still counting), and traveling with her husband, Glenn. Presently, Bonnie serves as a Church Service Missionary in the Intellectual Property Division at Church headquarters.

Be sure to read this book's companion *When He Shall Appear*— a joyful anticipation of Christ's Second Coming.